PRAISE FOR *HOTEL GOODBYES*

An extraordinary story of resilience. In his moving memoir, Stephen Thompson opens up about how he broke cycles of abuse, poverty, and neglect to build a better life. It's filled with lessons for anyone who's ever questioned their resolve.

—ADAM GRANT
#1 New York Times *bestselling author of* Hidden Potential *and* Think Again

This is one of the most powerful, vulnerable, and triumphant stories of perseverance and optimism I have read. It hits hard and hits quickly. Pain and determination. Hope and reality. The storytelling transports me to a familiar era long ago. It zooms in closely to personal circumstances and then zooms out for context to cultural, political, and economic events. It gives you a sense of the zeitgeist. I hope this connects with readers as quickly and deeply as it did with me.

—BERNARD BEDON, PhD
Vice President, Lead HRBP for Nike

Stephen tells his powerful and deeply personal story of over-coming hardship and adversity through sheer strength of will, determination, and courage. Showing incredible vulnerability, he opens up his life to fully expose the pain and intense trauma he experienced throughout his childhood. His journey reveals how from impossible circumstances the human spirit can persevere to achieve success and ultimately triumph. So many of us worked with Stephen for years and only saw the focused, talented professional building marquee companies not realizing where he started and what he faced growing up. Stephen's story is one of true inspiration.

—ARNNON GESHURI
Former Senior Director Global Recruiting at Google, Inc.

Hotel Goodbyes

RENO

THE BIGGEST LITTLE CITY IN THE WORLD

Hotel Goodbyes

STEPHEN JON THOMPSON

Forbes | Books

Published by Forbes Books, Charleston, South Carolina.
An imprint of Advantage Media Group.

Forbes Books is a registered trademark, and the Forbes Books colophon is a trademark of Forbes Media, LLC.

Printed in the United States of America.

10 9 8 7 6 5 4 3 2 1

ISBN: 979-8-88750-434-6 (Hardcover)
ISBN: 979-8-88750-435-3 (eBook)

Library of Congress Control Number: 2024907079

Cover design by Matthew Morse.
Layout design by Megan Elger.

This custom publication is intended to provide accurate information and the opinions of the author in regard to the subject matter covered. It is sold with the understanding that the publisher, Forbes Books, is not engaged in rendering legal, financial, or professional services of any kind. If legal advice or other expert assistance is required, the reader is advised to seek the services of a competent professional.

Since 1917, Forbes has remained steadfast in its mission to serve as the defining voice of entrepreneurial capitalism. Forbes Books, launched in 2016 through a partnership with Advantage Media, furthers that aim by helping business and thought leaders bring their stories, passion, and knowledge to the forefront in custom books. Opinions expressed by Forbes Books authors are their own. To be considered for publication, please visit **books.Forbes.com**.

ACKNOWLEDGMENTS

Penelope, your emotional support of this project was the key to me completing this book.

Fiona, thank you for believing there was a story to my madness.

Teri, your guidance and encouragement was everything.

Marnie, thank you for everything else.

To my family, thanks for allowing me to tell my story.

CONTENTS

CHAPTER ONE

Blue, red, orange...

I stare at the Rubik's Cube. Yellow, green, white...

I run my fingers over its hard, plastic edges. The 3-D puzzle has six sides, each with a different color consisting of nine movable tiles. The idea is to manipulate it until each side becomes a solid block of color. When you've done that, you've solved the Rubik's Cube.

I begin to twist it.

I manage a line of three greens on one side. I pull two orange tiles together on another.

But then my mind returns to the real problem I have to solve. I am nine years old and trapped in a motel room with my three younger brothers and my baby sister. It is Monday, we haven't seen our mother for two days, we have barely any food, and I need to do something.

But what?

* * *

It was Saturday morning when Mom left to take our clothes to the laundromat. Eugene had wet the bed again, and she gathered up the dirty sheets and our clothes and took off, mumbling angrily about how it would cost a dollar to wash and dry them. She had been out late the night before and was in no mood for our neediness.

At first, we waited. It wasn't unusual for her to disappear; she often left us for hours with me taking charge of Dana (age six), Eugene (five), Brian (three), and Tierra (one). The five of us sat on the huge bed or on the comforter that we had laid on the floor. We watched television and particularly enjoyed reruns of *Gilligan's Island,* a television sitcom about, ironically, a group of people shipwrecked and trying to survive on an island in the Pacific.

Tierra sucked on her pacifier, and I changed her diaper when it was needed. But at about 6:00 p.m. on Saturday, the power went out, the television and lights went off, and we were left in the dark. It was lucky that the heat stayed on since Mom had taken our clothes and we were only wearing underwear.

And there we were. Stuck. We breathed in the musty air. We knew that we had to keep the curtains shut so that no one could see in. Earlier that afternoon, the front office manager had called to ask when Mom was going to pay her bill. Not wanting to alert them to our presence—there were more of us than were allowed in one room—I made my voice sound like Mom's and assured the woman that the bill would be paid the following day.

Mom had left us a box of Nilla Wafers, so I doled them out, saving some for the next day. We had nothing to drink so I filled cups of water from the bathroom tap. But my siblings were tired of being trapped. Desperate to keep them quiet now that the front office was on our case, I did my best to distract them with made-up contests such as who could sit still or hold their breath the longest.

Eventually, they all fell asleep, leaving Dana and myself to trade theories on where Mom was and how long it would take for her to return. We didn't have any answers but talking about it made us feel better. Eventually, we must have fallen asleep, too.

Sunday came and went. There were only so many times I could ask my siblings to count the light bulbs in the room or the pictures on the walls. They were bored, hungry, and wanted their mom. We had no television and only a few toys. Tierra, the youngest, had a baby Chrissy doll that had no clothes and barely any eyes. Eugene had a Mr. Potato Head with no ears. Brian had a Hulk toy. Dana and I shared the Rubik's Cube, one that our mother had found after a customer left it at her table while she was waitressing a couple of weeks before.

For nearly a month, we had been living in the Super 7 Motel on East 4th Street in Reno near the MGM Casino. Motels were nothing new. We had lived in motels, shelters, run-down apartments, the Greyhound bus, and a car. We were used to sharing beds and sleeping on floors and, most of all, waiting around for Mom, who cobbled together a meager living through an endless merry-go-round of waitressing gigs, housekeeping assignments, and food stamps. Mom could never hold a job for long, so we were often hungry. Constant movement was the hallmark of our early years as we followed Mom as she followed whatever man she was involved with at the time.

The Super 7 Motel, with its fake wood paneling, faded brown plaid bedspread, and drop ceiling, was no different from the countless residential motels we'd stayed in before. It was one room with a dark bathroom and a small kitchenette. The motel had nothing that appealed to children except the dirt pile in the back corner of the parking lot where we played. None of us were in school. Mom was out most of the time so we either watched TV or dug around in the dirt pile. Life went on like this for weeks with Mom in and out, on her way back and forth to work, or out to party with her friends. Funds were at an all-time low.

I was in charge until Mom returned in the evening, hopefully with milk and a box of Frosted Flakes or something we could reheat in our small microwave. If Mom was in a good mood, or if too much time had elapsed since our last substantial meal, she'd take us to the local shelter for some hot food. When we first moved to Reno, we would frequently go to the downtown homeless shelter off 4th Street by the Circus Circus and Sundowner hotels.

The Reno-Sparks gospel mission served hot food every day. At the time, the Voyager 1 spacecraft was making its way to Jupiter, but there we were, standing in line with hundreds of others, freezing cold and waiting for hot turkey, soup, and warm bread.

By the morning of the third day, out of food and almost out of diapers, Dana and I agreed that we could no longer stay in that motel room. But I still hesitated when I picked up the dingy off-white receiver and placed my finger on the dial pad. Mom's face flashed across my mind as I recalled her constant mantra about not involving other people, especially white people, in our family business.

"Stephen, what happens in these four walls stays in these four walls," she would say. "I don't want you to talk with people about our lives. If anyone asks you questions, especially white people, I want you to value where we live and what we do. We are not less than others and people don't need to know anything about the way we live."

I can now see how Mom's betrayal was perfectly planned. She'd set it all in motion through years of molding me into a steadfast caregiver for my younger brothers and sister. She'd trained me to assume total responsibility for them as well as to display unwavering loyalty to her. For this reason, it took over forty-eight hours for me to finally alert someone of our existence and ask for help, forcing me into a decision that haunted me for years to come.

But I had no choice. My siblings and I could not remain imprisoned and foodless. We needed help and that was when I took a deep breath and dialed the front desk. When the front desk manager answered, I said, as calmly as I could: "There is a problem in our room. Can someone come by?"

I hung up and at first felt a wave of relief washing over me. I'd been working so hard to keep everything under control, and now, finally, I might be able to hand my burden over to someone else. But then another wave hit me, and this one threatened to engulf me. Guilt. I had betrayed Mom. What was going to happen? Would she decide not to come back for us now that I had done something unforgivable? Mom was clear that we keep people out of our lives and business. I had let her down.

Dana and I quickly wiped everyone's face and hands with a facecloth. Then we lined the kids up, sitting on the bed that dominated the room. Even though the little ones were hungry and cranky, they cooperated.

Suddenly, there was a knock on the door, and someone called out, "Front manager!" The little ones fidgeted; Tierra squealed and fell off the bed.

The person knocked again.

"Hush up, everyone," I said.

A key turned in the lock, and Dana and I looked at each other. As the door slowly swung open, light flooded the room and I squinted. The front desk manager, framed by the sunlight behind her, appeared almost angelic. The door had not been opened for forty-eight hours, and the air must have reeked with the fetid smell of body odor and soiled diapers. As her eyes fell upon five small children, the woman gasped.

"Mom's gone," I blurted.

The woman was in her midforties and petite with mousy blond hair that hung in stringy clumps. She wore faded blue jeans and a cream and red snowflake sweater. She glanced around the room and said, "I'll be back in a jiffy."

Dana and I eyed each other. My stomach churned. Maybe I should have waited another day? Maybe Mom was just around the corner? Maybe something bad had happened to her and she needed my help?

Minutes felt like an eternity elapsed, followed by a sharp knock at the door that made my heart beat almost out of my chest. I was embarrassed to be in my underwear, but I opened it anyway. The woman had brought two police officers. I had not expected to see the police. Their hands rested on their guns. I wasn't fazed. I had seen guns before. Still, I was breathing fast.

Were we going to get arrested? Had Mom done something awful? The officers were stony-faced and got right down to business, the shorter one peppering me with questions.

"Where is your mother?" he said sternly.

"I don't know," I said. "She went to the laundromat to wash our clothes."

"Well, when was that?"

"Saturday, but I am sure she will be back any time."

The officer looked at his colleague and back at me. "How old are you?" he asked.

"Nine," I said.

"Are you the oldest?"

"Yes."

The other officer spoke then. "When did you last leave this room?"

"Three days ago," I told him.

"What did you eat?" he asked.

"We had some water and a few Nilla Wafer cookies."

There was silence in the room between the officers and the front desk manager. The younger officer then changed his tone: "Well, let's get you out of this room and into some clothes," he said. "What's your name?"

"Stephen," I said.

Brian and Tierra began to cry. "You're okay," I told them. I lifted Tierra onto my hip. The police officers rooted through our things. Other than some trash, there wasn't much for them to see.

The officers wrapped blankets around us and marched us single file out of the room, down the hallway to the front lobby of the Super 7 Motel, and then outside. I was still carrying Tierra. As we emerged out of the motel, the warm sunlight felt good on my face. I looked around. *Mom? Are you near?*

As the police officers shepherded us toward a waiting car, fear gnawed at my stomach. They told us they were taking us to Social Services, but I didn't know what would happen after that. Our motel room, while it wasn't cozy, had been a familiar space. Now everything was unknown. My siblings stayed silent. Tierra and Brian had stopped crying. As usual, they all looked to me for reassurance and guidance, so I kept up a brave front and wore a faint smile on my face.

Eugene entered the police cruiser first, followed by Brian and then Dana. As the police officer shut the door, I walked around to the other side of the vehicle. Even then, I somehow expected Mom to run up and explain to the police that this was all just a misunderstanding.

Clutching Tierra tightly to my chest, I got into the police car. I took one last look over my shoulder, scanning the motel parking lot. *She can't be too far away.*

Inside the car, my bare legs stuck to the cracked black leather seat. As the door shut, I looked at my siblings. A faint scent of alcohol filled the air from a long-ago spilled bottle of beer. I had never been in a police car, and I felt like I was in trouble. Eugene was looking around, taking it all in. We had seen *Starsky and Hutch*, the cop show that was popular at the time, and I could see he was excited.

Brian leaned his little body into Dana, who gave me a blank look that communicated what we were both feeling. Then he turned his head and looked out the window. I looked up to the sky searching for a bird, a cloud, anything to take my mind off the shame I felt in front of the prying eyes of the gathered motel residents who stared at the spectacle that was my family departing in a police cruiser. Tierra was firmly encircled by my left arm but my right one, resting on the door's armrest, began to shake uncontrollably. *Can't let them see I'm nervous*, I told myself. But I was. I was nervous. I was ashamed. I was scared. I couldn't deny it any longer. Mom was gone and not coming back. Tears welled up in my eyes. I wanted to cry, to scream. *Maintain yourself. You can't let them see you upset. Be strong.*

I was a young boy. My main worry should have been how to solve the Rubik's Cube. But now my only toy was laying forgotten in a motel room. It was discarded. Left behind. And so were we.

CHAPTER TWO

*I*t had been several rough years before we arrived at that motel room in Reno. My birth mother, Brenda Milan Bell, was born on April 15, 1952, in Indianapolis, Indiana. She was the oldest of five children born to Francis Bell, my grandmother, whom we called "Nana." Brenda's father, my grandfather, was unknown to us. Nana had three children with this unknown man: Brenda, Ouida, and Eugene. Some years after that, Nana had two more children by two other men: Freda and Linda. I have very little information about Mom's childhood and upbringing. She didn't talk much about her mother and other siblings, except for her younger brother Eugene. She often spoke about him, and it was obvious that she loved him a great deal.

She moved around quite a bit. She lived in Indiana for several years and then spent some time in Boston, but eventually moved away from her family after high school graduation. She may have been hiding from someone or something. Overall, I can only assume that her childhood was not great, and that her early years failed to equip her with the wherewithal to deal with some of the curves that life would eventually throw at her.

On June 20, 1970, at the age of eighteen, Brenda Milan Bell married Stephen Earl Thompson, also eighteen, in Los Angeles, California. I was born exactly four months later, on October 20, 1970. My birth father disappeared quickly from our lives, and I never met him, speaking to him on the telephone on only one occasion. Other children soon followed for Brenda, fathered by two different men: Dana, born in 1973; Eugene in 1974; Brian in 1976; and Tierra in 1978.

Because I was the oldest child, Brenda came to rely on me for companionship in a way that I believe many young, single mothers do. I was the one she turned to as a confidant. Brenda loved to go out with her friends, and she would often ask my opinion about her appearance before heading out for the night. She was 5'7" with big brown eyes, a smooth complexion, and a curvaceous body that men were naturally attracted to, even after having had five children with three different men.

Beyond her physical appearance, Brenda was a passionate woman who held strong beliefs and spoke her mind. While she always enjoyed chatting with her girlfriends about the men in their lives, she also loved to discuss politics. There were whispers of her involvement with the Symbionese Liberation Army and the Black Panthers. She supported Jimmy Carter and hated Ronald Reagan, although this is not a surprise given that she was a Black woman living in poverty in the 1970s.

Although Mom neglected us in many ways, she paid attention to how we behaved and demanded obedience. All of us knew that if we didn't listen to her and follow her rules, she would punish us harshly. I credit Mom for raising me and my siblings to be extremely well-mannered and respectful. We did what we were told. My siblings and I grew up to be extremely polite, very nice, thoughtful, and measured in what we said. Over the years, the people taking care of us would comment on how polite we all were. I know it can be hard for people to understand, but I credit Brenda with this.

Brenda also passed along another important trait: the power of influence, the ability to get people to do something for you without their knowledge or resistance. Mom really knew when to turn on the charm and men easily succumbed to her will.

One man who fell prey to Brenda's charms was Augustus Miller, known as Gus. I first met Gus when I was about five years old. At 5'10" with a big barrel chest, thick arms, and a big Afro with an accompanying mustache, Gus embodied the epitome of a 1970s Black man, complete with rayon shirts and flared jeans. He was light-skinned with almond-colored eyes and a wide smile. A naturally charismatic guy, Gus had lots of friends. People were drawn to his charm, a characteristic that he would capitalize on in his later years as a preacher. Although not highly educated, Gus was a very persuasive man, and he exerted tremendous influence, even over my strong-willed mother.

Gus grew up in Sacramento, California, but had family near Youngstown, Ohio. Brenda had family there as well; both her mother, Nana, and her sister, Ouida, were living in Youngstown at the time. That is how Mom, Dana, and I ended up living there in 1975. I was five then and Dana was three. Gus was staying with his family in Youngstown when he met Mom, an alignment of the planets that would eventually lead to us being abandoned in that motel room.

Initially, Mom, Dana, and I moved in with Gus, who had a nice two-story home a few blocks away from Nana's. Over time, though, the house started to deteriorate, and eventually, piles of clothes and dog poop covered the floors. Mom and Gus loved to party, and soon friends and acquaintances who shared their love of heroin and Thunderbird wine filled our home. I didn't know what alcohol was, but I remember routinely finding bottles of the pale green liquid with a distinctive eagle on its label around our house. I also recall being given some of this to drink one evening and subsequently spinning in circles around the living room much to the amusement of Mom, Gus, and their friends. They kept rubber bands and needles in the bathroom for when they shot up. To me, this was normal.

All I knew was that the green liquid and the needles seemed to make Gus and Mom feel better and when they felt good, they would be nice to me.

I am not sure if Gus had a job. When we needed money, Mom and Gus hustled and stole. We were on welfare, and sometimes we would receive boxes of food from shelters. Mom and Gus also stole meat from grocery stores. They'd walk in, browse the meat case, then Gus would grab a couple of rib eye steaks while Mom grabbed something else. When she was pregnant with Eugene, she could fit several packages of meat inside her maternity clothes. Dana and I went along on these shopping adventures since we were a good distraction. While we ran up and down the aisles, the store clerks focused on our antics and didn't notice Gus and Mom thieving away. After we left the store, we'd head over to the drug house where Gus and Mom would deliver the meat to their dealer in exchange for heroin. We were never able to eat what they stole.

After getting high, Mom and Gus would fall asleep for days. While Dana was allowed to wake them, I was not allowed to disturb them at all. Gus always treated me differently from Dana. I think that's because I was the older child and had such a closeness to my mother, while Dana was just a toddler. When they told me to stay in my room, I needed to do just that or there would be big trouble for me. Gus made his dislike for me abundantly clear. On many occasions, I would spend the day in my room just hanging out by myself, totally isolated, until Dana came back from elsewhere in the house at bedtime. I wasn't at school. I just played with my toy cars.

When they had no drugs, Mom and Gus were in a terrible mood, and I was often the target of their rage. On one occasion, I got in trouble for horsing around with Dana. We were wrestling on the couch, and he knocked over a bottle of wine. It spilled all over, the red liquid seeping into the tan fabric. When Gus saw what had happened, he grabbed me by the shirt, dragged me to the small deck off the upstairs bedroom, and hung me upside down over the railing by my ankle. As I swung off the balcony, terrified and trying to avoid looking at the dark wood floors below me, Gus told me that next time he would drop me like a sack of potatoes. "Start acting right," he said. "I'm sick of your shit, boy."

All the while, Mom watched from their bedroom with a glazed expression. Nothing Gus did seemed to put her off. He possessed a magic that Mom couldn't resist.

Hunger was nothing new to me, but sometimes it was inflicted on me deliberately by Gus, not allowing me to leave my room even to eat. Dana would come upstairs to our room in the evenings and report that he had eaten a sandwich or even something from McDonald's. Often, I had not eaten for a day or two. Somehow even at the age of three or four, Dana felt guilty about my going hungry.

One night, when Dana returned to our bedroom after finishing dinner, I asked if he could get me some food. I hadn't eaten anything except some cereal the previous morning. Dana explained that there was no food downstairs, but that he had some leftover food in his mouth.

"Can I have it?" I asked.

He nodded and then carefully dislodged some food from his cheek and held it out to me in his small hand. Gingerly, I took the chewed-up bits of hamburger and bun, closed my eyes, placed it on my tongue, and swallowed. I was disgusted but ravenous. My growing body desperately needed nourishment.

"Thanks," I whispered, wiping my mouth with the back of my hand. "Do you have any more?"

Dana paused for a moment and then slowly nodded his head. He then regurgitated some food, spit it into his hand, and passed it to me. Again, I took the mashed-up food, placed it in my mouth, and swallowed, trying not to think about where it came from. Sometimes I would wake Dana up to see if he could do this for me. This type of feeding happened on numerous occasions as Gus abused me, and Mom did nothing to protect me.

❊   ❊   ❊

Gus and Mom sunk deeper and deeper into their drug haze. During this time, they had befriended a white family who lived next door who were nice and great cooks. A heady smell of fresh bread wafted through their kitchen whenever we entered their house. We were barely surviving; our house became impossible to live in, and Dana and I spent more and more time next door until we were eventually living there full time. Not surprisingly, Gus and Mom evidently ended up getting in a fight with these folks, and they kicked us out. Gus and Mom then got into a huge fight themselves and broke up. Mom took Dana and me to live with Nana.

Nana had a stable household, and by this time, two more young children of her own: Freda, who was three years older than me, and Linda, who was a bit younger than me. Nana's house was big enough to accommodate Mom and her three children (Eugene had been born by then). I have fond memories of playing with my aunts and getting to know my Nana. I have no idea what my mother's mental state was at this point, but we had warm beds to sleep in and, for once, I enjoyed plenty of food.

RENO

THE BIGGEST LITTLE CITY IN THE WORLD

Hotel Goodbyes

CHAPTER THREE

"*W*ho's that?" said Nana. "I'm not expecting anyone."

Dana and I were rolling our Matchbox cars across the floor when there was a sharp knock at the door. We had been living at Nana's for about six months. Mom crept to the corner of the window and lifted an inch of the curtain.

"Police!" she hissed and ran from the room.

I saw the dark uniforms of the police surrounding the doors and windows. Nana had no choice but to open the door. "Is Brenda Bell residing here, ma'am?" an officer demanded.

"Well, she's come to visit on occasion," Nana stammered, in what was certainly a white lie.

The officers showed Nana a warrant for Mom's arrest, and she allowed them to search her home. The officers came inside and told us children to sit quietly on the couch. I watched in silence as about twenty officers combed the house looking under beds, slamming doors, opening drawers, pulling aside curtains, and rifling through closets. They suspected that Mom was somewhere inside, and they were determined to find her. Mom had done something bad; I knew it. Nana repeatedly denied knowing where her daughter was. Technically, this was true, as none of us knew where she was hiding. After a long search, the officers accepted defeat and left.

I was unsettled as I watched the police cars drive away. Where was Mom? I knew she was still in the house. What did they want with her? Nana looked around and then finally called out, "Brenda, you can come on out now. Those men are gone."

A few seconds later, Mom sauntered into the living room as calm as could be and nonchalantly explained that she had opened the door that led into the small dining room and stood behind it. Because it opened onto a corner, and she was so thin, she was able to flatten herself tightly against the wall and hold the door such that it could not move. The cops must have assumed that there was no way a person could fit behind that door.

Nana asked Mom some questions, but she never explained exactly why the police were looking for her and seemed completely unfazed. Eventually, Linda started crying and Nana turned her attention to her young daughter and dropped the subject. I wasn't as easily distracted. I was frightened. I wanted to know why the police were looking for my mother. What had she done? Would they come again? I had an unnerving feeling that it had something to do with Gus. The fragile sense of security that had been briefly restored during our respite at Nana's house was now shattered.

* * *

Only later did I realize that my mother might have been involved in something more than just petty crime. During the 1970s, protest bombings were commonplace across America, with five bombings a day at one stage. I suspect now that Mom may have been involved. I remember hearing something about a bridge she blew up, and that the attacks were carried out by various radical underground groups that she had links to. Then again, she could have been guilty of many other things such as theft, shoplifting, drug use, child neglect, or prostitution. Still, I doubt twenty cops would have turned out just for that. Whatever she'd done, Mom was determined to get a hold of Gus, gather a few things, and hit the road. Eugene was still a baby, so she took him with her.

"Hey," she said, sitting Dana and me down. "Your dad and I have got to leave. But you can stay with your grandma. It'll be fine. You'll go to school. Be good boys. I'll come back and get you sometime later."

I stared into her eyes. "Gus is not my dad," I told her.

I loved my mother deeply and knew I would miss her. But I was glad to be staying in a familiar place with my loving Nana. Mom said that when we did see her again, she'd have a new house for us, toys, and even a new Huffy bike each. There was no big fanfare when the time came for her and Eugene to leave since she was still wary of being seen out in public. She simply waited until it was dark, gathered a few things, and left. Life continued. Dana and I continued to enjoy going to school and playing with Freda and Linda.

* * *

Things were blissfully uneventful at Nana's for a while, perhaps a year or more, until one day my Nana got sick and was taken to the hospital.

I can't remember exactly what happened, but eventually she died. I was desperately sad. Nana was one of the first people I really became attached to. In many ways, she was a more significant caregiver than my own mother, and I was much more traumatized by her death than I was by the ongoing absence of my mother.

After Nana died, Dana and I were sent to a foster home. The last night we slept at Nana's house we discussed what was going on.

"What will happen to us?" Dana asked me.

"I don't know," I said.

"Do you think Mom will come back and get us?"

"Yeah, I think so. She won't leave us by ourselves."

"When will she come?"

I didn't know. Neither Dana nor I had the answers. All we knew was that things were going to change, and change they did.

CHAPTER FOUR

I open my eyes and look to the left. I can see the faint flickering of a television and hear a cartoon playing. Maybe it's morning. Given how dark it is in the basement, it could just as easily be midnight. Children are asleep in the beds around me. The adults and just a few children sleep upstairs. I am an early riser and always wake first. I reach a foot outside the covers and snatch it back. It is a cold morning. A sliver of light shines through the basement window and onto the far wall. A beam of light from heaven? God scares me, but I pray anyway. If I am bad, I will go to hell. Am I bad? Maybe I am.

I sit up in my bed and wonder how long I have been in this home. Has it been weeks? Maybe it has been months or even years? The room smells musty, and I try not to breathe deeply. This place is nothing like Nana's. And now, not only my mom is missing but also Dana, who was sent to a different foster home.

Nana's house had been full of light and happiness. I think of her, my mother, and Dana. I try to recall them, but already their faces, their voices, have become blurred in my mind. I am six years old and feel like a prisoner of war (POW).

* * *

Years later, I would read Vice Admiral James Stockdale's story of being a POW during the Vietnam War. Stockdale was a naval aviator whose plane was shot down over North Vietnam in 1965, and he spent seven years as a POW. I was struck by his experiences of being held in small, dark, and cramped spaces. To keep his mind strong and prevent himself from going crazy, he would recount books he had read.

While I would certainly not compare my experience to being a POW, my bed under the stairs was certainly a dark, cramped space, and at six years old, I had no books to recall from my memory. I was frightened, despairing, and could feel myself fading—I couldn't remember anyone I knew. I was without my family, surrounded by people but completely alone.

It wasn't my first foster home. Dana and I were originally put in the same home, but they eventually separated us into different locations. It's hard to recall where I was and when. The various homes are indistinguishable. I kept to myself and nothing out of the ordinary transpired.

One thing I do remember is that it was around the time when the first *Star Wars* movie was released. All the boys in the foster home longed to watch it. One of the older boys had seen it, but I would not get the chance until years later. The kids in the home all had problems like me; many of them much worse, I'm sure. I got picked on a bit by the older boys and quickly learned that when I woke up the best thing to do was to stay in my bed and be quiet so that I would not wake anyone. I would lean my back against the wall, pull my knees into my chest and hug them tight, thinking of my mother, imagining that my knees were her that I was clinging to.

Sometimes I would start to cry.

When I first arrived at the foster home, I would cry every morning. This made the older boys punch me and tell me to shut up, so I trained myself to cry without making a sound. I had to be strong. I had to find a way to believe in myself. So, while I allowed myself to cry, I made sure that I appeared strong on the outside. I desperately had to believe that things could and would get better, that there was a life for me outside of this foster home. I began telling myself I could do it; I could survive. I told myself over and over that I believed in myself. I stubbornly clung to that belief and so, as I sat in the early morning dark, in that cold, musty basement, I rocked back and forward and silently implored myself: *Be strong. You will make it.*

I do recall the day I left that foster home. It was early evening when a young woman from Social Services knocked on the front door. We were finishing up dinner and it was my day to clear the dishes, so I went from the dining room to the kitchen where I could see beyond into the hallway. The woman stood in the small, dark foyer. She was tall with dark curly hair and was wearing a navy blue, two-piece suit with a heavy black overcoat. I heard her speaking quietly to Charlie, our foster father, who was a tall African American man in his late forties. I watched as he signed various forms that she presented to him on a clipboard. Then he glanced over at me as I was loading the dishwasher and beckoned me toward him. I closed the dishwasher and walked down the short hallway from the kitchen to the front door as the other boys snickered and whispered, assuming that I was in trouble.

"Yes, sir," I stammered.

"Stephen, this nice woman is going to take you to live with your aunt. So, go on upstairs and gather your things as quickly and as neatly as possible. I don't want any mess in that room. Just because you're leaving doesn't mean you can leave behind a pile of trash for the others."

I was confused and stared at him. Did this mean I was leaving for good? I knew better than to ask Charlie any questions. He had little tolerance for the questions of young boys.

"Go on. You heard me," he barked. He thrust a trash bag at me. By that time, I had moved to an upstairs bedroom and reluctantly climbed the stairs, looking at the fading and torn flowered wallpaper. It wasn't that I was sorry to leave; I was just anxious about what lay ahead. I entered the room I shared with three other boys and headed over to my area. It took a few moments for me to gather my few possessions and place them in the black bag. I looked out the window and saw a blue sedan parked in the driveway. I trudged back downstairs and followed the social worker out to the waiting car where I slid into the back seat, placing the black trash bag at my feet.

There was another little boy in the car. He was a few years younger. He seemed vaguely familiar to me and smiled at me tentatively. His happiness annoyed me.

"Who are you?" I snapped.

"Stephen, you remember your own brother, Dana, don't you?" chirped the social worker.

Dana? My mind reeled. This boy was smiling at me so brightly that he had to be someone I knew. Could so much time have passed that I no longer recognized my own brother? How much time had passed? Maybe only a year or two? I studied the boy. It was him! Dana had gained weight and filled out, no longer a toddler, but a little boy. I gave him a playful shove and grinned from ear to ear, elated to be reunited with my beloved brother, my closest confidant, and my partner in survival. As the car drove off into the night, I had a feeling that wherever we were going would be much better than where I had just been.

CHAPTER FIVE

1977
YOUNGSTOWN, OHIO

The social worker took us to the home of our Aunt Ouida. Somehow, even though she lived not far from us, we had rarely visited her. It turns out she didn't live far from the foster home either, and when the car pulled into her driveway, she was waiting on the front porch with a baby in her arms. Ouida lived at 150 Breaden Street in Youngstown. Today the house is dilapidated and run-down; the whole street is littered with boarded-up structures and overgrown lawns. But in the 1970s, Breaden Street was beautiful, lined with trees, and the homes featured neatly trimmed, thick green lawns. Ouida lived in a two-story, red-brick, and ivy-clad home with a wide front porch.

Ouida was in her early twenties and had long, curly hair that she wore naturally. She was of medium height and build and light-skinned with a ready smile and kind eyes. Although we didn't know her well, there was an air of familiarity and natural warmth. We walked up the steps of the porch, and she grinned widely at us, shifted the baby, and enfolded us in a big hug. It felt so good to be hugged. I hadn't realized how much I'd missed physical affection until Aunt Ouida wrapped her arms around us.

"Do you remember me?" asked Aunt Ouida.

Dana and I replied together that we did. I was so happy to see my aunt or anyone who wanted me. Ouida's voice and mannerisms immediately reminded me of my mother, which was a comfort. Dana and I walked into the living room and looked around the home. The front door of the colonial-style home opened into a center hall, like the ones you often see in movie sets in the Midwest such as *Groundhog Day* or *Planes, Trains, and Automobiles*. There was a big backyard as well. It was a charming home—warm and comfortable with four bedrooms and two bathrooms all centered around the expansive entryway and staircase.

Followed by the social worker, Aunt Ouida showed us to our room explaining that we'd be next door to our cousin who was expecting a baby. I took in the sight of the twin beds and matching wooden dressers with metal handles. I was excited to see that a stuffed animal had been carefully placed on top of one for Dana.

"How do you like it, Stephen?" asked the social worker.

"I love it!" I said, walking toward a smiling Aunt Ouida for another hug. She explained to Dana and me that our mom was traveling out of state. "She'll be back to get you soon," she said.

That night, as I lay on my bed, looking first at Dana and then at the ceiling, I felt as if I was finally home.

Ouida was married to Jerry, a great guy who epitomized the American dream. He had a steady job at the Youngstown steel mills, a nice car, a beautiful home in a lovely neighborhood, and a loving family.

Uncle Jerry also had a lucrative side hustle selling weed. I would watch wide-eyed as he counted out his piles of dollar bills. The fact that he was providing for his family sat deep with me. I was impressed, regardless of the source of his income, which I didn't totally understand at the time. I hadn't seen that quantity of money before and it would be a long time before I would ever see it again. But the memory of him doing that made an impression on me. At that moment, while watching Jerry, I knew I could do it, too. Not sell weed, but push forward, try new things, and believe in myself. I would take forward what I said to myself at that foster home: *Be strong. You will make it.*

The time we spent with Aunt Ouida and Uncle Jerry felt like a normal life. She took care of Dana and me as if we were her own children. We went to school and enjoyed home-cooked meals. Ouida was a great cook and, on the weekends, she would often spend all day preparing delicious dinners for us and friends who would visit. I distinctly remember one elaborate feast of Cornish game hens, which I had never tasted before. Ouida even let me try a little white wine, which, like most children, I found disgusting.

That summer of 1977 was really the first proper childhood summer that I ever had. Dana and I spent our days digging in the sandbox at the park, hanging with newfound friends, and swimming at the local pool, staying there until our waterlogged skin puckered from the water and our stomachs started to rumble. At that point, we'd walk home, eat a quick lunch, and then head straight back outside into the hot sun to play until the twilight began to settle. As we finished the last runs of our touch football games, Aunt Ouida would stand on the front porch and call us in for dinner. I can still recall her sweet smile and how she would lovingly pat Dana and me on the head as we gleefully bounded up the front steps and through the swinging front door. To most children, this would be completely unremarkable, but to me, these mundane but precious moments shine brightly.

While living with Ouida and Jerry, I attended first and second grades. I felt like I belonged in school and pushed forward with attitude. I was the first child in my class to learn and sing the national anthem in front of my class, which was no surprise given my love of singing. As bad as life was with Mom and Gus, I had heard the radio and sung along to it as often as I could. The songs I heard and loved were by Earth, Wind and Fire, Sly and the Family Stone, Marvin Gaye, and Stevie Wonder. The constant partying of Mom and Gus at least gave my otherwise dreary life a soundtrack. One song, *Always and Forever* by the band Heatwave, with its lyrics that promised undying love and care, meant a lot to me. I loved to sing and even wrote my own little songs.

I was also one of the best readers in my grade and was in the advanced reading class. Living with Ouida and Jerry showed me what success looked like: a regular life with a house, a family, and love. It felt so good to understand how important a family was to success. Aunt Ouida told us that she loved us all the time and both she and Jerry hugged us a great deal. Staying with them offered a reprieve from the combat of life with our mom, with Gus, or in foster care. It was as if we were soldiers on leave for a year and it was great to refill our tanks and recharge our batteries. We were going to need it.

CHAPTER SIX

After about a year and a half into our stay at Aunt Ouida's house, Dana and I arrived home from school one day as normal.

"Stephen and Dana," said Aunt Ouida. "How was school today?"

"Fine," we responded.

"I have some good news for you both. Your dad is coming to get you both and bring you back to California."

"Gus is not our dad," I said.

"I know, Stephen, but he is coming to get you both and bring you to your mom. Are you excited?"

Was I?

"Yes," I said. And I was. I wanted to see my mom. I did not want to see Gus. That night as usual, Dana and I sat and discussed our lives. I disliked Gus intensely and even though I'd initially forgotten my brother Dana during the months that we were separated, I had distinct memories of Gus, who only had been in our lives for a year or so. Dana, on the other hand, was too young to remember the bad times and was happy that he was coming for us.

A week later, Gus arrived. He was uncharacteristically happy as he explained that he was there to pick us up and take us back to California on the bus.

In order to keep Gus in check, I remarked, "We no longer get spankings."

"Is that so?" he laughed.

After we gathered our things, a ritual that was becoming all too common, we stepped out onto the front porch. Uncle Jerry gave Dana a big bear hug. "Be good," he told him. He gave me a hug and a high five. "Watch out for your little brother," he said.

Then it was time to say goodbye to our beloved Aunt Ouida. I'm sure our parting must have been painful for her. She had taken care of us like her own and was deeply attached to us. Of course, she had no choice but to let us go back to our mother, but I assume she understood the lack of care we'd suffered. I'm sure she was reluctant to send us off into an uncertain future. But if she felt that, she didn't show it. She just held us tight and for one last moment. I was still in a place where I was loved and cared for and where life was certain.

"You take good care of each other," she implored. "Remember, I love you. Never forget that you are good boys."

She gave us one last hug and kissed us firmly on our heads. Then we headed slowly down the stairs and into Jerry's waiting car. I was in a state of shock but as the car pulled out of the driveway, I managed to turn around and take one more look at the house where I had experienced a real childhood. I stared at it, not blinking, trying to gather all the good memories and loving care that it represented, hoping it would sustain me through whatever lay ahead.

With Gus, we took the Greyhound bus from Youngstown, Ohio, to Sacramento, California. As soon as we boarded the bus, although we were heading to the West Coast, the so-called land of opportunity, I felt conflicted, as if we were taking a giant step backward. I understood that we had left behind a stable and loving home and were going back to instability and chaos. I was filled with dread. As brutal as it sounds, in some ways, I had forgotten about our mom. After all, there wasn't much to miss about her or the tumultuous and terrifying life she'd given us.

Not long after we were alone with him, Gus became his normal self, no longer smiling like he was at Aunt Ouida's. He glowered at our harmless little boy antics and barely spoke to us. The trip seemed never-ending with stops in several cities along the way. Dana and I shared a seat throughout the entire trip. I managed to make friends with some of the other young kids on the bus as we played games and sang songs and traded snacks that we'd bought with money Gus gave us at the various bus stops. At least Gus was ensuring I was fed. But for how long?

We were on the bus for three days and two nights and as the various landscapes rolled by, I was torn. I wanted the life I had left behind, but the excitement I felt about seeing my mom was growing. It had been two years since she'd fled Nana's house in the middle of the night.

Finally, the bus turned off the 305 freeway. Dana was quiet as usual, his large brown eyes scanning the streets as the bus pulled into a run-down motel parking lot in Old Town, Sacramento. Gus herded us off the bus and toward a small, U-shaped motel complex. We followed him slowly. My heart was beating fast. I wanted to connect with my mother, but I didn't know what she would be like. Would she be the same confused mess she was before? Would she still love us?

All these thoughts and more rushed through my mind as our shoes crunched across the dusty gravel. For a brief second, as I turned and saw the bus pull away, I felt my opportunity for a happy family life was leaving me behind. Then, a door to one of the motel rooms opened wide, and Mom appeared. She ran at first, then slowed to a walk. The sun shone off her forehead and I noticed that her hair was very short. Her sleeveless, printed dress looked like it should reach to her knees, but it was higher at the front than at the back. Her belly was poking out hard at the front. Dana and I walked toward her. I scanned her face. She seemed different. I wondered for a moment if it was her.

Mom knelt and hugged Dana. He wrapped his arms tightly around her. Dana was still her baby. I looked at him, his head turned to the side, resting on his mother's shoulder with his eyes closed as if he were in heaven. She held him, savoring the moment, then after what seemed like an eternity, released him, and turned to me. There was a moment of assessment in her eyes but even though I had grown like a weed, there was no mistaking that I was her son.

I said nothing and just stepped forward. Even at such a young age, I was able to grasp that my experience with Ouida and Jerry had empowered me. I knew what I liked, what I didn't, and what I wanted. Mom hugged me and started to moan, a noise that only a long-absent child can elicit in a mother. And just like that, my love for her came flooding back. I felt my mother's heartbeat and breathed in her familiar scent. She held me for a moment and then wiped her eyes.

"I am so happy you are both home with me," she said.

Then she pulled us both into a hug, held us at arm's length to admire us, then murmured proudly, "My boys are back. My big boys are back," and squeezed us to her once more. I felt the hot sun beat down on my brown arms. Gus had not said a word.

Mom led us into a cramped motel room and the tension of my former life reached out of the dirty carpet and gripped me by the throat. Hadn't I been promised a new house, toys, and a Huffy bike? I was in California, so where was the beach? It took a few minutes for our eyes to adjust to the darkness after being in the blazing sun, but then I saw two small boys.

Mom introduced them as Eugene and Brian. I was confused. Eugene was now two years old and looked quite different from when I had last seen him at Nana's, when he was just a baby. Brian, whom I had never met, was a toddler.

I looked again at Mom's protruding stomach and realized she was pregnant again. Now there were even more people to take care of. My mind hurtled back into my old life, and I was afraid that I was being dragged down into the darkness, once more fighting for survival. That night, I wrote one final song in my head:

Lights are brighter than the oldest star
Lights are deeper than the deepest hole
If you really want to know
Lights light up my life
They give me hope to carry on my dreams.

It was a song of hope. I sang it out loud a few times. And then I stopped singing.

CHAPTER SEVEN

1978

SACRAMENTO, CALIFORNIA

"A...r...b...y...s...

"B...u...r...g...e...r K...i...n...g

"L...a...n...d P...a...r...k D...r...i...v...e"

I longed to read, but I wasn't in school and had no books, so I attempted to fulfill my desire for knowledge by deciphering street signs and billboards.

The six of us shared a single motel room with a single bed for a few weeks. Dana and I slept on the floor, while Brian and Eugene slept in the bed with Mom and Gus.

Even though neither Gus nor Mom was working, we had plenty to eat and spent most of our time hanging around the motel room and the surrounding parking lot. Mom asked us about Aunt Ouida and our school. I told her how we'd played and swam all day, how I'd been first to sing the national anthem in my class, and how I had become a good reader. If it meant anything to her that I'd been making good progress in school, she didn't show it. She also didn't mention anything about me going back to school.

Eventually, Mom and Gus found a house to rent, and we moved up the street from the motel to a small house with a yard bordered by a twelve-foot fence. We were among other similar homes, many of which were boarded up. The area was run-down and teeming with a few homes, parking lots, low-rent apartments, fast-food restaurants, gas stations, and residential motels. But at least we had a yard to play in. Dana and I played outside for hours: tag, hide and seek, and throwing a ball for a dog we'd recently acquired named Snoopy. But in no time, an old car was sitting on our lawn, the grass grew long, the house filled with piles of unwashed clothes, and Snoopy ran away.

Despite telling Gus that we no longer got spankings, he was back to his old habits. One time, he and Mom took Dana and me fishing with a friend of theirs at Folsom Lake. We enjoyed a decent day, and when we packed up and got in the car, I sensed that everyone was in a good mood and made a little joke, about what I can't remember.

"What did you say?" Gus yelled.

I had no idea that he was talking to me until the car screeched to a halt and he jumped out and yanked me from the back seat. He threatened to leave me by the side of the road if I didn't "straighten out." He told me to get back in the car and we drove off.

* * *

We were soon caught up in the idea of having a new sibling in the house and would take turns rubbing Mom's belly and putting our ears against it. When the time came for Tierra to be born, Gus took Mom to the hospital and a friend of hers came to look after us. Tierra came home to a house full of devoted brothers, but before too long, Gus made an announcement.

"I'm sick of your shit," he told my mother. "I'm fed up with taking care of you and your kids. This house is a pigsty, and I'm not living in it anymore. I need to find myself a new 1980s wife." There was an explosive fight, and he soon left the house. I watched from the kitchen doorway as my mom sat at the table and cried. It was hard to see her in so much pain, and it was the first time I had seen her display such a deep emotion that wasn't anger. I was reluctant to try and comfort her, but thought I better give it a shot. Then I stopped myself. I hated Gus and for years wished him gone. But now that he was gone, my mother was heartbroken. *Was it my fault?*

A few weeks later, Gus moved back in, bringing a young woman home with him. She had a young daughter and they lived with us for a few months. My mother began inwardly fuming as she flung pots and pans around the kitchen and openly raged at Gus for humiliating her. Although a formidable force when she wanted to be, my mother lacked the willpower to kick Gus out. And what real choice did she have, saddled with five young children? Gus provided her with companionship and some income, and I don't think she could face being on her own. Ultimately, this decision was taken out of my mother's hands when Gus and his girlfriend packed up their things and departed.

Mom was devastated and was never the same again mentally. Love gone bad can be like a tornado, leaving wreckage and destruction in its wake. When a tornado comes, folks go to their basements to wait it out. But when it came to the tornado caused by Mom and Gus, we were bystanders without a basement. My mother blamed us for Gus's departure. Partially anyway. I'm sure of that.

A few weeks later, we moved to Rancho Cordova, not far from Sacramento. I assume we moved there because Gus's brother Seal lived in that town. Seal was in the military and was stationed at the McClellan Air Force Base. Much to my relief, the area was nice, and I began attending the nearby White Rock elementary school. We lived on 2941 Grayson Way in the nicest house we ever lived in with my mother. This was the closest we ever had to a normal life with her. She got a job at Lucky's supermarket and that, along with food stamps and welfare, enabled us to survive. We went to school every day, and I even had a bike, admittedly only a broken-down Huffy, and my own room with a mattress on the floor.

Mom gained weight, a good sign that she was no longer using drugs. And in her attempt to bring some structure to my life, she reached out to my birth father, Stephen Earl Thompson. I had a brief, meaningless conversation with him on the phone, the last one I would ever have, and to this day I have never met the man.

CHAPTER EIGHT

1978
RANCHO CORDOVA, CALIFORNIA

*"Children almost always hang onto things tighter
than their parents think they will."*
—E.B. WHITE, AUTHOR OF *CHARLOTTE'S WEB*

I was curled up on the couch reading my school copy of *Charlotte's Web* and spellbound by the enchanting friendship of Charlotte the spider and Wilbur the pig. Charlotte seemed so calm and wise. I read on as she explained to Wilbur that she needed him to look after her children. Wilbur was a sweet soul, naïve and curious. He had no idea that soon he would never see his beloved friend ever again, the one who had gone to tremendous lengths to save his life.

I barely registered the bang at the door.

Bang, bang, bang.

I got up and went to the front door where Mom was peering through the distorted glass to see who it was. Then she opened the door, paused, screamed, and jumped into the arms of a man.

The man swung my mother around and then threw a large military bag onto the floor.

"Are you staying a while?" my mother asked him.

"Sure," he replied.

"Stephen, kids, this is your Uncle Eugene. My baby brother!"

All the kids had gathered around by this point, and Uncle Eugene gave us big kids high fives and tickled Tierra under her chin as my mom looked on proudly. He sat down, and my mother brought him a drink as they chatted. He was warm and charming, and we immediately fell under his spell as he shared the stories of his time in the US Air Force. He was fond of planes and told us about different fighter planes like the F-15 Eagle and the world's fastest plane, the Blackbird. For us young boys, Eugene's tales were thrilling, and he held us completely enthralled as he described his military exploits and globe-trotting experiences.

Eugene's presence lifted Mom. Life was hard for her as she supported five kids on her own by working a monotonous, low-wage job. She was lonely and spoke to me about many things, especially politics, even though I was only eight. She rarely spoke about her and Eugene's childhood. I got the sense that she'd wanted to get away from her life and her family. I guess she missed her sisters, but she knew she couldn't return to Ohio because she was in trouble with the law, and because by that time Nana had died. I think she always envied her brother Eugene because he was able to leave his family and join the military.

Not long after Uncle Eugene moved in, he met a girl called Shay, who had a couple of kids of her own. Mom quickly converted the garage into a bedroom for me so that the new kids could sleep in what used to be my bedroom. I didn't mind; I liked having Uncle Eugene there.

For a while, Mom really tried. I know she wanted a stable life for us. And maybe it would have happened if she'd connected with a different set of folks. Instead, even though Eugene seemed great at first, he and Mom started partying hard and she soon lost her job.

After a while of being unemployed and partying with Eugene, Shay, and their friends, Mom started prostituting herself to feed her reborn drug habit. Once again, our lives slid into the abyss.

One day, while Eugene and Shay were out, some men in military uniforms knocked on our front door. We watched from behind the curtains as Mom spoke with them on the front steps. The men looked stern, and it was obvious they were US Air Force officers looking for Eugene. They asked Mom a series of questions about her brother, his whereabouts, and recent activities. My mother, ever the loyal sister, flirtatiously answered the officers' questions, denying that he had been living there and pretending that she had neither seen nor heard from him in several years.

"Imagine that my own baby brother ups and leaves the US Air Force and doesn't even tell his beloved sister!" she cooed at the officers.

She continued to bemoan her "no good, no count" brother who didn't even have the decency to call her every now and then. The officers bought her story and walked back to their car. Mom joined us at the window and watched intently as their black Crown Victoria sped off down the street. She looked proud of her brother's ability to outfox the US military. Not long afterward, Eugene, Shay, and her two kids moved into their own place not far away.

* * *

"Steve! You all need to get the hell out of here!"

A man was shouting. I was sleepy but managed to open my eyes.

He yelled again. "You need to get out and back to your mom's place down the road. Your mom ain't here, and you can't stay here either."

I realized Uncle Eugene was the one shouting at me. He shook me violently.

"You can't stay here; you have to GO." He was screaming now. Bewildered, I quickly sat up and began looking around for my shoes and socks. I was only wearing underwear and a T-shirt.

"Okay, Uncle Eugene," I said quietly. "I'll put on my clothes."

"No!" He stood over me. "You better put your shoes on and fast. You ain't got time to put on your shirt or pants."

It was a summer evening when Mom took us to visit Eugene at his new place. He had a three-bedroom apartment in a big complex with a large swimming pool. It was much nicer than our house and included a hobby room where Eugene kept all his model planes. As the night wore on, my siblings and I fell asleep on the floor of Eugene's hobby room, and it was there that several hours later I was woken by the sound of him yelling at me. I was dazed and could barely register what was going on.

Apparently, Mom had left us at Uncle Eugene's house to go to a party at a friend's house several miles away. Now Eugene was demanding I leave and go and find my mom. It was 12:00 a.m.

I nodded at him. *Why was he so mad at me? What had I done to provoke such rage?* I got my shoes and socks on, stood up, and went toward the door. As I reached for the doorknob, Eugene grabbed me by the shoulders and spun me around. "Wait. Where do you think you're going?"

"You told me to leave so I'm leaving, Uncle Eugene," I said. I was confused and concerned that I didn't seem able to manage my uncle's anger. His commands were ridiculous, but I was trying to obey him and calm him down for the sake of my sleeping siblings. I had learned by this point in my young life that when someone is raging at you, the best strategy is to not ask questions and simply do what you are told. I had been in countless situations in which drunk or high adults had given me nonsensical commands and I had enough wherewithal to figure out what to do to survive. But Eugene's irrational volatility was like nothing else I'd ever experienced.

"You ain't leaving them with me," Eugene shouted, gesturing at my brothers and sister curled up together on the carpet. "Naw, naw, you gotta take all these kids with you. I ain't no babysitter."

I bent down and began to shake my brothers and sister awake. One by one, they sat up, rubbing their eyes and Tierra began to whimper.

Eugene stood in the corner, fuming, and smoking a Kool's cigarette while I frantically tried to find shoes and socks. As the minutes wore on and I tried to find clothes for everyone, Eugene began to pace like a panther. "Hurry up, boy," he sneered. "I already told ya, you ain't got time to get all their clothes on. Just find their fucking shoes!"

Shay came into the room then and asked Eugene what he was doing. He told her to shut up and go back to bed. She just stood and stared at me with sad eyes. Finally, having found shoes for my younger brothers, I wrapped Tierra in a small blanket and herded my siblings toward the door. Eugene shooed us out. "Go on, go on. Get yourselves out of here," he said, following us out of the room, down the stairs, and out of the front door where he stood with his arms folded. "And tell her she better not come round here no more. I don't need any more of her shit."

Eugene's words barely registered. It was the early hours of the morning, and I was only eight years old. I was out on the street with my four siblings. I needed to know where my mom was and how I could get everyone to her as safe as possible. And at that moment, Eugene, satisfied that he was no longer burdened with our presence, went back into the apartment and slammed the door, leaving us in our underwear in the dark and chilly air.

I lifted Brian into my arms as Dana lifted Tierra into his. "Hold Eugene's hand," I told Dana as I began to shepherd my family down the street. Uncle Eugene lived on a busy four-lane street lined with retail stores and gas stations on one side and a large open field on the other. We might have been safer walking beside the retail units, but there was too much light on that side of the street and people would have been able to see us. I wanted to walk on the other side where we wouldn't be noticed. However, by the open field, there was no sidewalk, so we walked on a strip of asphalt, separated from passing vehicles by a thin white line. As the gravel crunched beneath our feet, my siblings were eerily silent. Even at their young ages, they understood the severity of the situation and followed my lead, doing what I'd instructed. They dutifully trudged along beside me as I positioned myself on the extreme left-hand side of the road's shoulder, dangerously close to the oncoming vehicles, so that I could keep them safe.

With every car's passing, my fear that one of them would hit us grew and I hurried the four of them along, wanting to get off that road and out of the darkness as quickly as possible. This was no small feat for the little legs of my younger brothers who desperately tried to keep pace with my quickening stride. My heart raced and my mind churned as I tried frantically to remember where my mother's friend's house might be, my panic interrupted only by the occasional drivers who would honk their horns at us.

My mind reeled as I tried to figure out whom I was angrier at: Mom for once again neglecting us in her all-consuming desire to get high, or my Uncle Eugene, who had been a role model but who had now thrown five small, vulnerable children out into the night. I was scared, and I was mad. Adults could not be relied upon, I thought, and it was thanks to them that we were being humiliated, parading down the main road in our underwear, and in danger of being hit by a car.

Then, from the corner of my eye, I noticed cars slowing down and passengers' faces shocked as they registered the pathetic tableaux of five young Black children marching along the street in the middle of the night in their underwear. I felt deeply ashamed and tried to ignore them. These feelings of shame only steeled my will to get us off that road and to safety as soon as possible. I averted my eyes and ignored any potential offerings of help. At one stage, a car pulled over and the driver, a middle-aged Black man, opened his passenger door and leaned out: "Hey there," he said. "It's kind of late. You know it's dangerous to walk along a busy road like this. Do you guys need some help?"

My reply was polite but curt. "No. We're fine," I said, carrying on walking. The man watched us for a few minutes, and then closed his door and drove off. For all I knew, he may have been well-meaning, but I was not putting my family in that car.

We continued our journey and, after what seemed like a couple miles, we arrived at mom's friend's house. By some miracle, I managed to find it after only having been there once before. We approached the front door and Dana, Eugene, and Tierra collapsed in a heap on the front steps as Brian slumped in my arms. They were just as relieved as I was.

We knocked on the door and eventually a small, white woman wearing bell-bottom jeans and a multicolored tunic swung the door open wide, calling out, "Come on in...." Then her voice trailed off, and without saying a word, she slowly moved to the side so that my mom could get a full view of us. My mom could not believe what she was seeing. "My babies, oh my poor babies!" she screeched, running toward us and gathering us in her arms. She was genuinely emotional as she and her friend wrapped us in blankets and gave us warm milk. Initially, I retreated from my mother's embrace, unsure if her anger was directed at me or at Uncle Eugene. It was quickly obvious that she was furious with her brother. I had seen her angry on many occasions, but this was on an entirely new level. She could barely speak, "How could ... What did ... What kind of ... They could have been killed!"

Mom's friend Pam spoke to me: "Steve, what happened, honey? Weren't y'all s'posed to be staying with your Uncle Eugene?" I nodded, hesitated, and then began to explain what had happened. As I spoke, Mom became more and more angry. She balled her fists up and kept hitting the sides of her hips with them. "You do understand, Steve," she raged, "that what your uncle pulled tonight is totally unacceptable and downright dangerous. He put you all directly in harm's way and I will personally see to it that he never, ever comes near any of you again!"

Pam took us into her spare room so that we could go back to bed. While the little ones immediately drifted off, I tossed and turned, listening to Mom screaming at Eugene on the phone. It seemed that Uncle Eugene was trying to make it seem like it had been my idea, but fortunately for me, Mom wasn't buying any of it. I lay in bed thinking about Wilbur and Charlotte. If only, like Wilbur, I'd had a kind and loyal friend to protect me that night. But I was quickly learning that no one was coming to save me. I was going to have to save myself.

CHAPTER NINE

Hearing a crash coming from the kitchen late one night, I shouted to Dana, "Stay with the kids!" and ran to check what was going on.

Somehow Gus had found out about our middle of the night excursion and, as a surprise contender for a "Father of the Year" award, was livid. Mom let him in, and they began talking. Shortly after that, Uncle Eugene turned up. He had been drinking and probably taking drugs. He and Gus got into a fight, and someone must have fallen on the kitchen table because it collapsed, which is what caused all of us kids to wake in panic.

"Get out of here! This is none of your business!" Mom screamed when she saw me coming toward the kitchen. Hearing the fear in her voice, I slowly backed out of the kitchen and into the hallway. I ran back into the bedroom to check on Dana and the little ones. Just then, I heard a loud bang followed by my mom screaming and then the front door slamming.

As soon as I heard the door slam, I ran back to the kitchen and found Eugene on the floor writhing in pain as Mom held a kitchen towel to his leg. Tears were streaming down her face. There was a pool of blood on the floor next to Eugene, and the lower half of his jeans on his left side was turning dark red. I had never seen so much blood in my life, and I didn't know what to do. Mom yelled at me to help her carry Eugene out to his car. He was moaning in pain and swearing about "that nigga, Gus."

We put Uncle Eugene in the car, and while I stayed with the younger kids, Mom drove him to the hospital. It turned out that the bullet had just grazed his leg and he was released later that evening.

I went back inside the house and tried to clean up the kitchen, sweeping up the broken glass and putting the chairs away. There was a lot of blood on the floor, but I decided not to touch it. I would let my mother figure that out herself. I walked into the back room where the kids were asleep, with Dana watching over them.

"Did you see the blood on the floor?" he asked me.

"Yes," I said.

"That was crazy."

We laid down and waited for Mom to come home.

＊　＊　＊

After the altercation between Gus and Eugene, Mom began drinking more and I began to try and keep track of how much money she was bringing home. She would go out at night and come home very late and very drunk. On many occasions, Mom would be so hungover that we were required to stay in bed all day as she could not manage to get up and care for us.

Each day, my mother told me whether I was going to school or not. But some days, when she was too out of it to take care of my siblings, I stayed home anyway. No one at the school seemed to notice.

One morning, I woke up to find my mother splayed out in the middle of the hallway. She had passed out, either on her way to or from the bathroom, with her underwear and pants hanging down around her legs. I gingerly stepped over her as I headed to the bathroom. When I was finished and was heading back down the hallway, Mom looked up at me from the floor and said, "You go back to your room and stay there for the rest of the day. I don't want to see any of y'all until the sun comes up tomorrow morning!" I knew not to disagree with her when she was in that kind of a mood. My siblings and I stayed in our bedroom, where we played quietly and did not eat until the next morning when we woke up starving.

On countless occasions, random men spent the night at our house. Mom was not only partying but continuing to sell herself for money and drugs. Sometimes if she was having sex, she would send us into the backyard and lock the door. We would have to stay in the yard all day. It was a bug-infested mess thanks to the baby pool that had never been emptied and contained stagnant, festering water that attracted all sorts of insects. We were bitten and hungry, but we waited outside until we were told to come back in. If we needed the toilet, we peed up against the fence. There was a row of metal shopping carts lined up in the backyard—Mom's attempt to provide us with some toys to play with. We pretended they were a train and spent hours playing with them, waiting for the men to leave.

I realized what was going on when she started spending time with a rich, married man. He would come over or she would go to his house and, without fail, as soon as she left him, she suddenly had three or four hundred dollars in her purse. I would check what she had in her purse and knew that if she had about three hundred or so, we'd be okay, for a while. Anything less than that and we were in trouble. This money would not last long, and she would visit him again. We even accompanied her once to his house, which was on a golf course. She went into a back bedroom with him for a few hours while we sat on the couch and watched television with his maid watching over us.

On several occasions, the landlord came to our house and asked me if my mother was home. I was nearly always there looking after the younger kids and would tell him she was working. It was obvious that she was struggling to pay the rent. I sometimes had money, from a birthday present or from some change that I'd found, which I would use to buy a Pepsi or some gum, normal kid stuff. I always hid any money that I had in my drawer, but Mom would still find it. Eventually, once again, the house was ruined, which my mother blamed on us kids, and we had to move out. We packed a few clothes into some black trash bags.

By this point, it was clear to me that the adults who were moving in and out of my life cared only about drugs and alcohol and didn't care about us kids. I was painfully aware that we were poor and not doing well at all. I no longer felt sorry for my mom. In my eyes, she was weak. Depression, addiction, and mental illness weren't words I knew or understood yet. What I did know was that I was the one doing the best for my siblings. I was the one who shepherded them down that dark road in the middle of the night after being kicked out by Uncle Eugene. I was the one looking after them day after day. At some point, I realized that I was going to have to take complete care of all my siblings. I was going to have to become the pack leader.

CHAPTER TEN

BETWEEN RANCHO CORDOVA, CALIFORNIA, AND RENO, NEVADA

*W*hen I heard my mother talking to her brother Eugene about gambling, I realized she was convinced that she could pursue her dream of riches and a better life in the Silver State. The Nevada state song is *Home Means Nevada*, which is ironic since our eventual move there was a move into homelessness. For the moment, however, we pretty much lived on the Greyhound bus, shuttling back and forth between Rancho Cordova, California, and Reno, Nevada—about a two-hour drive—dragging our black trash bags behind us. We still lived in Rancho Cordova, but when Mom wanted to gamble and hopefully "get lucky" she dragged us all to Reno.

The Greyhound bus station in downtown Sacramento became very familiar to us. At first, we were enthralled by the fact that each seat in the bus station had a miniature television. To begin with, our mother provided us with quarters, which we would excitedly deposit into the side of the televisions. While waiting for the bus, we stayed out of her hair and enjoyed our favorite TV shows like *Tom and Jerry* or *Bugs Bunny*. But as the trips continued, Mom ran out of quarters and those fantastic TV screens became nothing more than the blank back of a bus station seat. The novelty of our bus excursions soon wore off and this traveling thing became less fun.

In addition to the lack of quarters for cartoons, my mother never had enough money for our actual bus tickets. She fell back on her hustling skills, buying tickets for Tierra and Brian, while Dana, Eugene, and I would try to sneak around the bus driver and board the bus while he was distracted collecting tickets. Usually, this feat was easily accomplished as many bus drivers were older men for whom the shuffling of bags and organizing of anxious passengers was all-consuming. They seemed to be more focused on making sure that no one pickpocketed them rather than keeping track of how many children a Black woman was herding onto the bus. So, while the driver was loading bags into the baggage hold, we would cut into line, glide up the bus stairs, and take a seat in the back. Occasionally a younger, slicker bus driver would catch us and chase us off the line. Then we'd have to hide and wait for another opportunity to stowaway. Our mother took great pride in our ability to score seats without paying and would routinely brag to people about how good we were at getting free bus rides. In fact, this was the only time I can remember my mom being proud of us.

I assume Mom was getting money—either from welfare or prostitution or both—then going to Nevada to gamble with it. Some nights, we would just sleep on the bus until we got to Reno or back to our house on Grayson Way in Sacramento. On rare occasions, we would stay at dingy kitchenette motels in Reno. Overall, though, our trips to Reno were accompanied by a growing realization for Dana and me that things were not normal. Our meals were catch as catch can, none of us were in school, and Mom had no regular job. I understood how desperate our situation was becoming.

Not long afterward, as our bus pulled into Reno, I was gripped with anxiety as I knew that we didn't have a place to stay or food to eat. How was Mom going to manage it this time? As we got off the bus, she strode into the bus station where she quickly gathered up our things that the driver had unloaded and marched us out the other side and toward The Sands Casino. *What is she up to now?* I wondered. *Was she really going to herd us all into a casino?* I hoped she would not as it was always so hard to pass by the all-you-can-eat buffets with their mouth-watering array of fresh fruits and vegetables alongside steaming trays of Alaskan King crab legs and hot grilled steaks. But Mom led us past the entrance to The Sands, across the street and toward a building I hadn't seen before. I stared at the large letters: Reno-Sparks Mission. I had no idea where we were.

Mom ushered us inside and we were immediately greeted by several nice middle-aged white women. They made us feel right at home, asking our names and ages, and showing us to the dining room where they gave us hot soup and warm bread. My siblings and I were wide-eyed as we watched scraggly bearded men wearing shoes with holes in them mingling with women with unwashed hair and layers of threadbare sweaters. Children yawned over their plates as their mothers eyed them to make sure they took seconds and cleaned their plates, unsure of when they might get a hot meal again. We were no different, so we ate our fill and then Mom followed one of the women into the front office while I kept one eye on the little ones and the other on my mother. *Where were we going next?*

The sun was setting, and I feared that we'd be going back out onto the strip where Mom would wander aimlessly in and out of casinos while Dana, Eugene, Brian, Tierra, and I—too young to go inside the casino—would wait and watch the crazy behavior of desperate gamblers, drunks, drug addicts, and prostitutes.

After about fifteen minutes, Mom sauntered toward us, escorted by one of the mission workers. "This lady is going to take us to a place where we can stay," my mother said. We followed her outside to a waiting van and clambered in, holding our trash bag suitcases.

After a short drive, we arrived at a nice house on the outskirts of the strip, where an older white woman with graying hair and glasses was waiting on the front stoop. She smiled as we walked warily up the sidewalk. "Welcome," she said warmly turning to open the front door. She led us into the house and up a short flight of stairs.

"What are we doing here, Mama?" Eugene asked.

"We're going to stay here, honey," Mom said. "Come on y'all. Let's go and find our beds."

We excitedly carried our bags up the stairs. There was a large room with two sets of bunk beds and another with two twin beds. It was simple but cozy. "I think you'll be comfortable here," the woman said. "Let me know if you need any extra blankets and pillows." Mom nodded at her and smiled and then we set about choosing our beds and settling down for the night. Dana gleefully bounced on the upper bed of one set of bunk beds while Eugene snuggled in down below. Brian and I shared the other set. Brian was young and I thought he might fall off the top bunk, so I settled him in to the bottom bunk and climbed up to the top bunk. Mom tucked Tierra into the single bed they were sharing.

Words can barely do justice to the relief I felt at having a comfortable bed, clean sheets, and a warm room to stay in after months of being on the move, always on constant alert and ever vigilant. It was obvious we were desperate, and men would be eyeing us and hitting on Mom, ready to take advantage.

* * *

After a couple of nights, Mom managed to find a temporary place for us to live in Reno and she even got a job at a famous soul food joint downtown called the Squeeze In. I don't remember why we couldn't move back to our house in Rancho Cordova, but I guess Mom had not been paying the rent and so we had no choice but to stay in Reno. We began staying in a variety of weekly motels on West 4th Street—some better than others—before we moved into another apartment.

With Mom waitressing, we were getting by, but I was plagued by horrendous diarrhea that lasted several weeks. I was in severe pain and spent hours in the bathroom, probably extremely dehydrated. Intense stress and terrible food were most likely taking their toll. We mainly ate canned foods, Wonder bread, Miracle Whip, bologna, sausage meat, and canned tuna fish. Rarely did a fresh fruit or a vegetable pass our lips. Mom didn't notice that I was sick or if she did, she didn't care.

RENO

THE BIGGEST LITTLE CITY IN THE WORLD

Hotel Goodbyes

CHAPTER ELEVEN

"*I*'ll be home for Christmas. You can plan on me…"

Bing Crosby's voice oozed from the car radio as I watched the snow falling on the windshield. If it hadn't been for the DJ, I wouldn't have known it was Christmas Eve.

We were living in a car—a two-door Datsun hatchback that belonged to Mom's new friends, Fred and Grace. They stayed in the front of the car, sleeping in the two bucket seats with Grace's four-year-old daughter. The six of us lived in the back on a bench seat.

The snow crunched as Mom came running back toward the vehicle. This time, she was actually trying to find us a hotel room to sleep for the night. When she opened the car door, the cold air hit me in the face. She clambered in behind Fred and perched beside me. "Any luck?" he asked.

"Nope, they're booked through New Year's," she said.

Silence filled the car. My legs were dead from Brian laying on top of them. I shifted to try and get comfortable. Mom gave me a look.

"If you move again, I'll punch you," she said. Fred, Grace, and Mom discussed how much gas they had and how often they would need to run the engine to keep some warmth in the car. I listened to them, watching as the snow from my mother's hair melted and dripped onto my legs. I couldn't feel a thing and I was grateful for that.

✳   ✳   ✳

"Turn over and go back to sleep!"

When, inevitably, Grace and Fred broke up, he and my mom hooked up. We got a motel and since we were sharing one room, I would wake to the sound of them having sex. She would instruct me to go back to sleep. I would try, but even though this was normal to me by then, I was still furious and disgusted.

Somehow, maybe via a well-meaning receptionist at the motel, a social worker named Debbie Husselcuss came into our lives. Debbie was a Black woman in her midthirties. She was well-meaning and kind but also no-nonsense. She placed us in a shelter and enrolled me and Dana into Glenn Duncan Elementary School on Montello Street in Reno. The neighborhood consisted of low-income housing and was a rough area, but Dana and I attended the after-school club provided by the Boys and Girls Club of America, and things were okay.

I was so happy to be learning again, but because it was so obvious that I was poor—due to the fact that I was getting free lunches and wearing thrift store clothes—the other kids didn't like me. This didn't bother me much. I was used to people not liking me. Maybe I was depressed and couldn't care less. Or maybe, I was so used to not belonging anywhere that it didn't even cross my mind that I might somehow be accepted by other kids. I guess it makes sense that I wouldn't be able to relate to other kids and perhaps they sensed that.

One day on the playground, I got into a fight over marbles. The other kid was winning and got me onto the floor where he started punching me repeatedly. I was writhing in pain when suddenly someone punched the other boy from behind. My attacker fell off me and I was able to scramble to my feet. A wave of relief swept over me as I turned around to see Dana standing there, a proud grin on his face. My little brother had come to my rescue. As always, we could only count on each other.

* * *

Soon Mom started to act odd. She was often spaced out and one day when we were visiting Debbie in her office, Mom was sent to a separate room. Debbie went through her usual routine of asking us how we were doing, where we were living, whether we were attending school, and so on. Then, after about ten minutes, she leaned forward and said, "You know, your mommy is having a hard time right now and she isn't feeling so well. She needs to get some rest and so she is going to stay in a hospital for a little while where she can get better."

"What does that mean for us?" I asked. "Where will we live and who's going to take care of us?"

"You'll be going into foster care," Debbie said.

Mom was admitted into the Truckee Meadows mental hospital, and we knew that she was getting treatment for drug and alcohol addiction.

I don't recall much about the foster home we stayed in, but I do remember regular, supervised visits with Mom, who would come to school to see us. I was excited when I knew I'd be seeing her, and it was great to be with her as she was so different from before. She was very tender as she affectionately held us and earnestly implored us to remember how much she loved us. She was always eager to hear our news—what we were doing in school, the latest books we had read, our favorite games, etc. I think that because she was no longer under the influence of drugs and alcohol, she could see the precarious plight of her children. For once, her mind was clear, and she'd had some time to think deeply. She even remembered my birthday, and that I liked music, and bought me a tape of The Muppets album. I didn't know too much about The Muppets, but I enjoyed learning and singing along to the songs. "If you remembered your homework like you did your songs, you'd be doing really well at school," she told me. I took the tape home and listened to it in my bedroom.

Within a few months, we were back with Mom and on the move again, this time to Sparks, Nevada, a middle-class city with very few Black folks. We moved into a two-bedroom apartment with one bathroom and a small kitchen. I remember one evening when Mom made a meal for us, which was unusual. She asked me to go and get some salt, and because I had no money, I went out and stole some from a nearby restaurant. Mom was surprised by my acquisition, but not mad at me for stealing.

I started a new school, although I can't remember the name. But, despite Mom's best efforts, our lives quickly slipped back into the old routine, and I started skipping school to care for my younger siblings so that Mom could work. Those days at home with my siblings were long. We didn't have TV, so they mostly just ran around the yard. On the days when I could go to school, did my teachers ask me where I'd been? I don't know. But if they had, I guess I would have told them that Mom was sick. Nobody was connecting the dots.

After a while, Mom began coming home later and stopped bringing us food. Money was tight and Mom hated it when my brother Eugene wet the bed, meaning that she would have to spend money at the laundromat. It wasn't his fault. He was only five. On one occasion, she demanded that we all punch him for wetting the bed, to which Dana and I refused.

Things got so bad financially that mom once again invited a new man to come live with us to help her pay bills. He was an older Black man who, at first, seemed quite nice. He would tell us jokes and make us toys out of newspapers and cardboard that he found lying around and, to my knowledge, he never harmed any of us. Still, it was unsettling to have a stranger living with us.

RENO

THE BIGGEST LITTLE CITY IN THE WORLD

Hotel Goodbyes

CHAPTER TWELVE

1979
SPARKS, NEVADA

"You look good, Mom," I said.

Mom was going out for the night with Holly. Holly was our neighbor in Sparks, and when we could no longer pay the rent, we moved in with her. Holly was white and had no children, and she and Mom would go out at night looking for men.

That evening, I put my siblings to bed and then lay in my mom's room watching TV where I drifted off. It was my mother's laugh and a thumping sound that woke me. She was drunk, I realized. But then I heard a man's voice, low and whispering. I shuddered. Where was Holly? And who was this guy? Before I had time to move, the two of them stumbled into the bedroom.

"Steve," my mom whispered, her breath stinking of cheap liquor. "Get your ass up and outta my bed. You know you ain't supposed to be sleeping in here. Go on and get on up outta my bed." With that she toppled face down onto the bed. As she did so, the man lay on top of her and began kissing her neck. I scooted over the edge of the bed and went into the other bedroom where I fell asleep next to Dana.

The next morning, I awoke to the sound of Tierra babbling in her crib. I rolled over and picked her up, and then grabbed a bottle of milk out of the mini refrigerator in the kitchenette and handed it to her. I watched as she drank her milk, staring up at me with her big brown eyes. I was exhausted and couldn't remember getting into bed with my brothers. But then it came back to me. Gripped by anxiety, I put Tierra back in her crib and gently pushed my mother's door open. There was no one in the bed except her and I wondered if I had imagined her bringing a man home. Holly didn't seem to be around either.

Mom slept for a long time, so I got the kids cereal and toast and parked them in front of the TV. Then, at around noon, Holly knocked on the door. I guess she had forgotten her key. I let her in, and she nodded her head toward Mom's bedroom.

"Is she awake?" she asked.

"Nope," I said.

Holly went in and woke Mom up and I listened as they chatted about the previous night and giggled. The two of them spent the rest of the afternoon laying on the bed, smoking cigarettes and planning their next night out.

A couple of nights later a new man named Will began staying with us as well. Holly didn't seem to be about. Will was jobless and homeless and clearly saw us as a meal ticket. Mom and Will partied and spent most nights in a drunken haze. I didn't like Will because he was hardly making our lives any more stable and tried to keep him away from my siblings. I always felt it was my responsibility to protect my younger siblings from any new man in the house. In Will's case, it was easy since he displayed no interest in us and only wanted to get high or drunk and then have sex with my mother.

* * *

I stood frozen at the sight in front of me.

My mother whimpered and wiped a bloody tear from her cheek. "Honey," she said, "just go on back to bed. It's nothing. I'm okay. Really, I am. Just a little misunderstanding."

My mother's screams had woken me, chilling me to the bone. They weren't the regular sounds of her having sex or partying. She was hurt. I heard several loud thuds of crashing furniture, and something hit the wall. My brothers and Tierra woke up. "Dana, lock the bedroom door and do not let anyone in except for me or Mom," I said. Then I grabbed my wooden baseball bat from the corner of our bedroom. I crept out of our bedroom door, which Dana shut behind me. Then I ran to my mom's door, pushed it open, and, wielding my baseball bat, screamed, "Leave my mother alone!"

Will had his hands around my mother's throat. She was on her back on the bed and blood was pouring from a gash on her forehead. The bed was in shambles, and a table lamp lay broken on the floor; glass was everywhere. My mother's hair was wild, her dress was up around her waist, and her head was slumped to the side. Her legs bent at the knees, and she attempted to scramble backward and out from under Will's asphyxiating grasp. Will, still with my mother's throat in his grip, looked at me and said very calmly, "Son, sometimes you just need to beat a woman."

My mother began to cry. I was paralyzed, desperate to hit Will, but terrified that doing so would put my mother in more danger.

"Stephen, it's okay; I am okay," my mother said. "Just go back to bed." I backed out of the room, my bat now slumped at my side, and retreated. The noise from my mother's bedroom quieted to her occasional whimpering and Will's hushed angry tones. I climbed back into our bed, lay down next to Dana, and cried hot, bitter tears. Dana turned toward me. "Go back to sleep," I told him.

Things deteriorated quickly then. Mom, Will, and the five of us trekked from run-down motel to run-down motel. We were desperate and rarely ate. Then one day, we went downtown to the welfare office. I thought nothing of it as we had been there many times before. Running was prohibited so, while we waited, Dana and my brothers played a game of surreptitious tag. Tierra sat on my lap drinking her bottle as Mom looked around anxiously, tapping her foot, while Will wandered off in search of a Coke machine. The place had several counters and windows accompanied by rows and rows of chairs filled with sad and despondent people. The frustration and hopelessness were palpable. It was hot, crowded, and noisy as lots of school-aged children were aimlessly milling around, even though it was a weekday. Countless babies sucked on pacifiers as Black and white men traded stories of their latest misfortunes or acts of bravado while the women gossiped about their relationships and the latest hair products.

After a short while, a woman nodded to Mom from behind one of the counters. Mom grabbed Tierra and placed her firmly on her hip as she strode to the window, hissing at me to keep an eye on my brothers. I watched as Mom engaged in an intense conversation with the welfare counselor while Dana, Eugene, and Brian continued their game of walking tag. Mom lingered at the window for quite a while, occasionally glancing over her shoulder. Then she turned to us and snapped: "The counselor needs to see all of y'all. C'mon, c'mon, don't make me waste her time."

Dana and the other two stopped their game immediately and ran over to her. Mom hustled them to a side door that led into a back office. I furtively gathered up our things and followed behind. At that moment, Will came striding around the corner. As the office door opened, a young woman stood up from behind her desk and began frantically ushering us into her office as Will called out, "Brenda! Brenda! Wait. I'll come with you."

No sooner had he said those words than a huge man with a badge walked up to him and spoke into a walkie-talkie saying, "Okay, it's him." Mom pushed Dana, Eugene, and Brian into the office, but I lingered in the doorway for a few seconds watching intently as four police officers ran across the room and swarmed Will, one of them twisting his arms behind his back and handcuffing him. Will struggled to free himself, yelling, "Damn you, Brenda! This is some fucked up shit. Let me tell you about that woman. You got the wrong person. She should be the one in handcuffs." I heard his voice trailing off as I turned to walk into the office to join my family. As I did so, my eyes caught Mom's and we stared at each other for a good long while. I thought of the brutal attack in her bedroom and understood that our mother had done what was necessary to free us from Will's literal and figurative stranglehold. She had done what needed to be done, which brought her a measure of respect in my eyes.

We never saw Will again. We were placed in a safe house where there were other women living, as well as a person that was responsible for making sure we had groceries and decent meals and took care of the home. We attended school and Mom got a job. Things were good for a while, but after a few months we moved out. Maybe Mom had broken some rule, or we may simply have reached the limit of our allotted time there. But it was from there that we ended up at the Super 7 Motel in Reno, and it was from there that our lives would change forever.

CHAPTER THIRTEEN

1980
SUN VALLEY, NEVADA

After our mom abandoned us in the motel room in Reno, the police took us on a fifteen-minute car ride to the Department of Child and Family Services. A tall Hispanic woman with warm, brown eyes greeted us at the door. She told us her name was Rita. Although she looked tired, she seemed kind and quickly got to work trying to find clothes for all of us. She then spent a good deal of time talking to me, trying to piece together our story and complete her paperwork.

I tried to explain what happened. "Maybe we should call the motel to see if Mom came back for us?" I suggested.

Rita continued writing. "Hmm," she said.

The boys and Tierra were busy playing with the few toys that littered the corners of the office. They occasionally looked at me, checking to see if I was still there. After what seemed like an eternity, Rita informed me that they were sending us to La Casa, a temporary shelter for children. Rita left the room, and I called Dana over.

"Do you think that's the right thing to do?" he asked. "What about Mom? You know she's gonna be mad when she finds out about the police."

"She's not going to know. Don't worry," I told him. "I think this is the best thing for us to do. We can't take care of the little kids on our own anymore."

When the van arrived to take us to La Casa, Rita motioned for us to join her by the front door. Dana and I went over, then I nodded to the little ones to join us. My heart raced but I played it cool. Tierra toddled over, sucking her thumb, and clutching an old teddy bear she'd found. I scooped her into my arms and headed down the stairs to the waiting van.

Located in Sun Valley, a suburb on the outskirts of Reno, La Casa was a big Spanish-style home of beige stucco with wood trim and a terracotta-tiled roof. The house was surrounded by trailer parks. Compared to the city of Reno, Sun Valley was a relatively cheap place to live. The van pulled into the small driveway, and a man dressed in jeans and a faded sweatshirt walked down the front steps toward us. He had curly brown hair and a neatly trimmed beard flecked with gray. The van came to a stop, and the driver got out and walked around to the passenger side to open the door for us. We sat perfectly still for a moment, taking it all in, then I motioned to Dana to get out and for the others to follow him.

The man with the beard came over and introduced himself as Dave. We followed him into the house where we met his wife, Joanne, and together they showed us around our new home. My siblings were wide-eyed at what seemed like a castle, compared to where we had been living. In the front of the house was a large living room. From there, we went through a well-equipped kitchen and into a huge family room. I had never seen anything like it. Sliding glass doors led to an outdoor patio, which led to another multipurpose room. All the bedrooms were on the second floor. There must have been eight or ten bedrooms in total and although the house was huge, it felt very welcoming.

Dave and Joanne explained the basic rules. We were to be in bed by 8:30 p.m. and there was no eating in our rooms or rough play anywhere in the house. They showed us to a bedroom that had two sets of bunk beds and a toddler bed for Tierra. I was relieved to know that we wouldn't be separated. I wasn't sure how the little kids would have handled being apart.

We went to the dining room for lunch. I loved sitting at a table to eat rather than eating off a cardboard box while sitting on a motel room bed. Joanna and Dave brought out lots of different foods on platters. Having not eaten anything but Nilla Wafers for a couple of days, we were famished. But before we ate, I thanked Dave and Joanna, and then nodded at the others to begin. The boys dived in as I helped Tierra while I ate. The food was good and the rare sensation of being full was magical.

At bedtime, we enjoyed the simple routine of taking showers and brushing our teeth. We had not brushed them in months, and I am sure they needed a scrubbing. Joanna changed Tierra's diaper, said goodnight, and then left the five of us alone. I held Tierra, rocking her back and forth in my arms while I covered her ears with my hands, so that she would drift off. The others lay in their beds.

"Stephen," Brian said. "Do you think Mommy is coming back?"

"Yes," I replied, "but we are going to stay here for a while."

"Steve," said Eugene, "I like this place, and the food is really good."

"I know. I like it too," I agreed.

Dana said nothing.

When Tierra was sleeping, I laid her down in her crib. Then I got into my own bed, turned toward the wall, and let silent tears roll down my cheeks. Sorrow was like a creature inside me and now that creature was ripping me to shreds, clawing at my chest, desperate for release. Before, I'd never had any doubts that Mom would eventually come back.

"We live in a foster home, but she's coming back...."

"We live with grandma, but she's coming back...."

"She's going to an insane asylum, but she's coming back...."

"She partied all night, but she's coming back...."

I knew it was different this time. She wasn't coming back and that's what broke me. I could lie to my brothers and tell them Mom was coming back. But I could no longer lie to myself.

* * *

I had been accustomed to taking charge of my siblings for a long time and continued to do this at La Casa. For example, the kids would not eat until I gave them a silent signal to do so. This was noted by Dave in my official file that I would read many years later. He described how we "ate like a pack of wolves, looking to Steve as the leader." Gradually, though, I began to defer some of my parenting duties to Dave and Joanne. I trusted them and we all began to enjoy some semblance of normality.

The day after we arrived, I was enrolled in Sun Valley Elementary School. It felt normal to me to go to a new school and make new friends. I was like an army brat who constantly moved due to his parents' next deployment. But I loved to learn and going to school was important to me. And despite the interruptions to my education,

I made progress. I loved reading stories and having them read to me as well.

We stayed at La Casa for about four or five months, enjoying plenty of food, warm beds, and playing outside, where we built forts and played tag. In many ways, it was a happy time. It was a relief not to be shuffling from apartment to motel room or endlessly waiting in undesirable places for Mom to return. We had regular meals and consistent shelter.

But I felt as though I had betrayed my mother. And although we were all getting used to her absence, I couldn't quite quell the feeling that she might return someday, that we would live with her again, and that our lives would change back into what they had been before. After all, it wasn't unusual for her to be gone for long stretches at a time. Maybe she'd returned to that motel room and, finding it empty, was out somewhere looking for us. I wondered if I would be in trouble if she did eventually find us. I was also torn by my feelings for her. Despite her many shortcomings, she was my mother. It was very hard to come to terms with the fact that she was gone. Mom was on my mind, and I yearned for her. But at the same time, I did not yearn for Brenda. I wanted a mom, but I did not want Brenda to be that mom.

RENO
THE BIGGEST LITTLE CITY IN THE WORLD

Hotel
Goodbyes

CHAPTER FOURTEEN

Life at La Casa was good, but like most good things in my life, it ended too quickly. Finding foster families willing to take on five children was quite a challenge, but our social worker Debbie managed to place all of us with a Black family—two sisters, Katie and Marjorie, who lived next door to each other. They were both single, middle-aged women who also happened to be Seventh Day Adventists. They lived in Hidden Valley, a middle- to upper-class neighborhood in Reno where they each had their own home. In between them lived their grandmother and altogether the three women had three big properties and a lot of land.

Tierra and I lived with Katie while Dana, Eugene, and Brian lived with Marjorie. Katie had two children of her own: Stacy, who was about my age; and Monique, who was about a year younger. Who their father was, I never knew. Other foster children came and went, including John Kinsey, another Black boy, who was also about my age. John was short with tight, kinky hair. He smiled constantly, revealing a large gap between his front teeth, and was very good with people. He and I soon became good friends.

Each morning, Katie left to go to church where she worked in the office. Marjorie worked nights as a nurse. John and I would walk over to Marjorie's to call for Dana, and then the three of us would walk to the bus stop together. We attended Roger Corbett Elementary School. At the end of each day, we hung out together at Marjorie's again until 6:00 p.m. when Katie got home and then we'd go back to her house for dinner. Tierra, Eugene, and Brian were at home all day with Marjorie since they were too young to go to school. Both Katie and Marjorie were extremely strict, which after our anything-goes lifestyle under our mom's care was hard to get used to.

* * *

"You want to steal my food? You need more to eat? I'll give you more to eat. I'm making you some 'food for thought' tonight."

We had woken that morning to the sound of yelling and when we got to the kitchen, we saw Katie's daughter Stacy sitting at the table, her face wet with tears and swollen from crying. She had taken some extra pieces of bread and shared them with us. Katie was furious as that was a big violation of her rules. All of us stared at Stacy, wondering what her punishment was going to be, and back at the foster home that evening, it was worse than we could have imagined.

Katie had made it abundantly clear that no one could ever have more food than they were given, no matter how hungry they were. There was no shortage of food in the house, but we could only eat what we were allocated. Katie designated Stacy responsible for feeding us and after she had done so, Stacy then ate with Katie and Monique. In the morning we would get a bowl of cereal or oatmeal with a cup of milk. Tierra would not eat much of hers, so I would finish her leftovers. My big meal of the day was the free hot lunch that we received at school because, at dinnertime at Katie's, we only had beans and rice, sometimes with some kind of vegetarian meat substitute. No matter how hungry we were, we would only get one helping. This policy did not affect the girls in the house as much as it affected the boys as we were growing rapidly. Many nights we were still hungry, but Stacy was under strict orders not to give us any more food. She had to adhere to this rule as Katie kept meticulous track of all the food consumed in the house.

That evening, Katie summoned us to the table, which was unusual. But it was clear that she had not forgotten her threat to give Stacy some "food for thought." We had no idea what she was going to do, but we knew it would be something bad. Katie seemed to enjoy the attention, and it was clear that she wanted us all to witness Stacy's humiliation. First, she mixed together peanut butter, salt, and pepper. Next, she stirred in cooking oil. That didn't seem all that bad. But then she opened the cabinet underneath the kitchen sink and took out a bottle of bleach and a can of Comet cleaner. Was she going to make Stacy scrub the sink? No. My jaw dropped as I realized the full horror of Katie's plan. Slowly, deliberately, she poured in bleach and a tablespoon of Comet into the peanut butter mixture. All eyes turned to Stacy, full of pity. She looked down, tears slowly rolling down her face, not daring to utter a word. Having finished stirring the mixture, Katie then spread it liberally on two pieces of wheat bread. She then plopped the sandwich on a plate and shoved it in front of Stacy.

"No one is going anywhere, y'all," she snarled. "We're going to watch 'Little Miss Who Steals Bread' have some food for thought." Terrified that we would be next, none of us moved an inch. Stacy gingerly picked up the sandwich and held it to her lips. She hesitated. Katie shoved her head forward. "Go on," she said. "You're the one who is always complaining about being hungry." Stacy took a tiny bite and chewed for a few seconds, unable to swallow. Her tears became a river as she chewed and chewed, finally spitting the food from her lips. But Katie was relentless and made Stacy eat it again.

Time stood still as we watched poor Stacy struggle to finish the sandwich, dry heaving and almost choking with each consecutive bite. Stacy was already treated like the black sheep and servant of Katie's family and now it seemed she was considered even lower than even us foster children. Stacy threw up all night long but seemed OK the following morning. This was not the last "food for thought" Stacy endured during my time at Katie's.

* * *

Katie thought she was doing God's work. Her Bible was never far from her side, and it completely influenced her strict point of view and how we spent our time. From sundown on Friday to sunset on Saturday we were all involved in church-related activity. On Friday nights, Katie would have us doing Bible study, which meant reading the Bible for hours, as well as memorizing scripture. We would then have Bible races to see who could locate certain biblical passages the fastest. Friday night ended with an hour of prayer.

The whole of Saturday was spent in church, that being the sabbath in the Seventh Day Adventist church. We got up very early to ensure that all our chores were completed while Katie prepared food to share at a potluck meal. We would then drive to one of two churches. At the first church, on the west side of Reno, nearly all the parishioners, apart from us, were white. At the second church, in nearby Sparks, the congregation was almost all Black. The Sparks church was much more spiritual, and its members shared a closeness and affection with one another that was not evident in the other church. I loved going there for the good food and lively entertainment. The church in Reno, on the other hand, was much more aesthetically pleasing and comfortable as its parishioners were wealthier than those who attended the Sparks church, but it was more subdued and emphasized scriptural doctrine. The church sessions were shorter in Reno, which was a plus, but it was awkward to be one of the only Black families in attendance. After church on Saturday, if we'd been good, we might be able to watch *The A Team* on TV or go to a friend's house.

I had questions about everything, but we were forced to accept religious doctrine. The emphasis on doing good deeds and not sinning was lost on me. Did we not, as young children, demonstrate goodness? Had we not endured tremendous suffering in our young lives? I read the story of Job and of his suffering, and it seemed to me that God asked an awful lot of his disciples. I was not comparing myself to Job, but it was painfully obvious to me that religion was asking me to believe in something that might not be of any real help. The more I read of the Old Testament and Revelations, the more it became clear that I was being scared into believing in the Almighty. To me, Christianity seemed to be mostly about sin and punishment and it would be many years before I understood true Christian ethics.

On Sundays, we spent our time working around Katie's house. Her large yard was full of scrub brush and huge swaths of tough, ropy weeds. If you got in trouble, you were required to pull weeds. But these were not typical backyard weeds. The weeds in Katie's yard were four to six feet high and we would have to stay out and pull them for up to four or five hours at a time, then drag them around to the front of the house and place them in piles for eventual removal.

Many a Sunday was spent this way beneath the hot, sizzling Nevada sun. I hated it and thought it was abusive.

As time went on, my contempt for Katie only deepened. Marjorie's and Katie's own children had piano lessons but we foster kids had none. It was a tiered system. And to further enforce her authority, Katie had a large German shepherd named "Jaco" who seemed to be trained to attack anyone other than Katie and her daughters. I loathed that dog with its loud, deep bark and its glistening dagger-like teeth. Jaco had the privilege of sleeping in Katie's room. Each night, Monique would bring the dog in from the yard, running to keep up with his long stride. As she did so, we would shut our doors tightly, not daring to set foot in the hallway. The heavy chain around Jaco's neck rattled as he bounded up the stairs before he strode into Katie's bedroom. The dog was obviously there to protect her in case of intruders, but he was also a fearsome deterrent to any young child who was scared in the middle of the night and in need of a foster parent. None of us dared risk a possible encounter with Jaco and, therefore, if we were upset or having a nightmare, we had to remain in our bedrooms and console ourselves.

The whole time I lived at Katie's, I felt extremely tense. She constantly watched me, scrutinizing my every move. I became tremendously self-conscious and felt as if nothing was my own and that I was simply a working boarder in her home. School, once more, became my escape. As Dana, John Kinsey, and I made our way to school each morning, making money became our obsession. We were always talking about how we could make some money, and I still carried the memory of Uncle Jerry's weed deals that gave him and his family such a great standard of living. We'd somehow sneak off to a shop and steal strawberry-flavored Bubbalicious gum, which we then sold in school for twenty-five cents apiece. The other kids thought our gum was expensive, but one little girl said, "It's expensive but maybe these kids need it." Even the kids around us knew what was going on.

* * *

I loved learning. Like many schools in Nevada at the time, Roger Corbett Elementary School looked like an airport hangar. It was situated on a large property with soccer fields and a basketball court. It was comparable to a small community park and was well groomed and kept. The student body was largely middle class and white, like the general population in Reno. I began attending during the late fall, a couple of months into the school year. When I first arrived, the administrators asked me questions about my previous education and current grade. I explained that I'd been in fifth grade at the last school I had attended, but the principal decided to test me to see what level would be best. I sat with a kindly young teacher in the cafeteria for two hours. She gently explained the questions, focusing on reading comprehension and mathematics. Afterward, the principal explained to our social worker, Debbie, and me that I was at third-grade level for reading and fourth grade in math. Two years before, I had been reading *Charlotte's Web*, which is appropriate for fifth graders, so I had clearly fallen behind during those years shuttling back and forth between Sacramento and Reno.

Interestingly, the test also indicated that I was at an eleventh-grade level for listening comprehension. Both the teacher and the principal were surprised at this and said they had not seen anything like it before. Thinking about it now, it makes sense. From an early age, my survival had depended on my ability to listen to and carefully analyze what adults were saying to me and then try to navigate the precarious situations in which I found myself.

Based on my skills in listening comprehension, the principal decided to place me in the fifth grade. She then said she would take me to my homeroom. I felt very nervous as I walked past all the doors until we stopped at Room 127, where the principal knocked first and then swung open the door, revealing rows of neatly lined-up desks and walls filled with artwork. I looked around the room, taking it all in, and immediately noticed the absence of any other dark faces like mine. The students put down their pencils and fell silent as I walked to the front of the room and the principal cheerfully introduced me to Mrs. Wood, a medium height, heavyset woman with a warm and ready smile. Mrs. Wood welcomed me, introduced me to my new peers, and then asked if I would like to sit at a table with the others or have my own desk. I told her that I would prefer my own desk since, being tall, I knew that the little tables would be uncomfortable for me. I took my place at a desk at the back of the room and Mrs. Wood continued her lesson, explaining to the class that we were going to be reading *Where the Red Fern Grows*. I loved the family in that book. They had their challenges, but they stuck together and didn't split up when things got hard.

Mrs. Wood became one of my favorite teachers and someone whom I remember fondly. My attention was kept rapt by her wonderful reading voice and her ability to make books come alive. She was also good at explaining difficult concepts. During my time at Roger Corbett, she transformed my life with her colorful descriptions of everything from trees to trains to tadpoles. Sweet-smelling like a grandmother, Mrs. Wood was cheerful and full of life. I felt as if I could do anything in her class. To a child in my situation, a teacher can be a true gift. All the talk about whether teachers actually make a difference is lost on those who want to measure success solely by metrics and accountability. Mrs. Wood must have seen something in me. She realized I was smart, if not necessarily book smart. My experience with her laid a strong foundation that served me well all the way through high school and into college.

RENO

THE BIGGEST LITTLE CITY IN THE WORLD

Hotel Goodbyes

CHAPTER FIFTEEN

1981
RENO, NEVADA

I wanted to entertain people, but it was a part of my personality that I had never been able to explore. So, when I heard that the school was putting on a play, I decided to try out.

I didn't stand out academically, so I also figured that this was another way for me to accomplish something. With my mom, I worried about how I would survive each day. With Katie, even though she was a tyrant, I at least had stability, which meant that I had the brain space to think about other things. The play was about a kid trying to do something meaningful to get into heaven. The story was great, and I felt I would have no problem standing in front of people and reciting my lines.

I took the script home and began memorizing the lines so that I could audition for the lead role. I whispered the lines quietly, and since Katie placed a premium on learning and preferred that we keep quiet most of the time, she approved.

The next day, I was a little nervous as I entered the backstage area of the theater, and hearing a student reciting his lines in front of me didn't help. His name was Robert, and he was a skinny, good-looking boy with a solid tone to his voice. I did notice, however, that he stumbled over a few words and needed one of the teachers to feed him a prompt or two. He finished his lines and returned backstage as the teachers applauded. A few of the kids waiting to audition told him, "Way to go."

Then it was my turn. "Stephen Thompson," a teacher called out.

"Here," I shouted. I strode confidently onto the stage, smiling at the teachers as I began to recite my lines. I gave it my all, remembered every word, and won the part. It turns out Robert also won the part, so we then had to compete to see who would perform for the parents, which was considered the more important audience, and who would perform for the students. After two weeks of practice, we performed a final dress rehearsal in front of the fifth-grade classes to determine the ultimate winner. I was chosen to perform for the parents, and I was elated as it was one of the few things I had ever won.

The performance went well, opening with me walking out in front of the audience, looking around, and passionately asking, "What do I have to do to get into heaven?" Lots of people congratulated me on my performance, including Katie, who had come to see the play, along with some of the friends that I had started to make at school. Mrs. Wood gave me a hug and told me, "Good job."

* * *

With the play over, the summer of 1981 was upon me, and it was miserable, full of attending endless church services or pulling weeds in Katie's backyard. I'd had enough and was even more despondent when I met my teacher for the upcoming school year, Mr. Scott, who was cold and uninspiring. The atmosphere in the foster home, with Katie bearing down on her daughters and treating us foster kids as little more than staff, was oppressive. I complained to Debbie, who was still my social worker.

"This is your life," she told me. "Quit feeling sorry for yourself. You're lucky anyone wants you guys. Suck it up and learn to make the best of this situation. At least you have a roof over your head, a warm bed, and adequate food. It could be a lot worse."

Today, I understand what she was trying to do for me. She was telling me that this was my life and I had to deal with it. Acceptance of your situation, rather than fighting it, can lessen your suffering—a powerful message, but one I would only appreciate later. At the time, when she said those words to me, I was furious. I was done with the way my life was. I had reached my limit for chaos. I longed for a better life, a real home, a real family. The only time in my life that I had felt relaxed, like a normal child, was when we were living with Aunt Ouida and Uncle Jerry. That was what I wanted. I wanted normality. I wanted a life where kids stayed in the swimming pool until their skin wrinkled. I wanted a family. I knew that I needed a family if I was going to have a good life.

These were the days when people only had landline telephones and you remembered the phone numbers that were important to you. On one occasion, Katie asked Dana and me if we knew Ouida and Jerry's phone number. We did and she said we could call them. Jerry was home and it was great to catch up with him. He thought we were living with our mom, until we explained about Katie. He said Ouida was away, out trying to find us. As kids, those were pieces of the puzzle that we simply couldn't put together. Was Ouida with our mother? Were the two of them planning something? Looking back, it's possible that Ouida had gone to see her sister to try and encourage her to come and get us, but perhaps our mom had refused, saying that we were better off where we were. But we just didn't know.

Nothing came of that phone call with Jerry, and the system we were in was not protecting us from the cruelties inflicted upon us at the hands of Katie. The system, despite its best intentions, was failing us. Fortunately, there was never any plan for Katie to adopt Tierra and myself. The authorities were still looking for our mother. But if she ever came back, she would have to pay a fee for us being in foster care. The idea that she would pay money to get us back was ludicrous. The policy is a major stumbling block to families trying to get back together. Even if our mom had managed to get off drugs and alcohol and tried to be a better person, she wouldn't have had the money to purchase our freedom.

CHAPTER SIXTEEN

People were living better lives than mine. And I knew it. Things had to get better and be better, for me. I had to do something different and take a risk. I had to get out of Katie's home.

I had mentioned to my friend John Kinsey that I had to leave. He and I were close and would often get into trouble together and be punished by having to pull weeds. John was an old hand at running away and would get on the road a couple of times a year. He and I planned our escape from Katie's. I wanted Dana to come too, but after careful consideration, I decided that he would be better off staying behind at Marjorie's. I thought it was too much for him to be out in the streets with me and John. Plus, I'm not saying that life was easy for Dana, but his foster home was better than mine. I was taking a risk, but I didn't know what the risk would be for Dana. I calculated that leaving him behind was safer for him. And of course, Tierra was too young to leave the house and, as just a toddler, she did not suffer from the same abuse as me or even Katie's own children.

The morning of escape dawned. Every morning, we followed the same routine. We woke up, made our beds, washed, brushed our teeth, dressed, and then went downstairs for breakfast. After we'd eaten, we caught the bus to school. But this particular morning was different. John and I hid in the bushes and waited until all the other kids had caught the bus. Then we walked quickly to Katie's house—she was at work—and went through the side door into the garage where she kept two large freezers. We took some frozen bread. We didn't care much about getting into trouble and having to eat "food for thought" as we thought we would never see Katie again.

We didn't really have a plan, but John suggested we head over to Meadow Wood Mall, where we could get some food and drink. It was five miles away, but we didn't mind as we had all day. We arrived at the mall hot, sweaty, and tired and headed into a couple of convenience stores where we easily stole some candy and a few drinks. No one seemed to notice us or find it odd that two young boys were hanging around the mall on a school day. This lack of attention empowered us, and we were pleased with what we were getting away with. We left the mall and spent the day meandering around Reno. Then, as dusk began to settle over the city, we decided to make our way to John's old foster family over in Sparks. After several hours of walking, we finally arrived at their house. It was late when John knocked quietly on the back door. No one answered.

"Knock again," I told him. "They'll soon wake up."

"I don't know," John said. "Maybe we better not disturb them."

"Where are we gonna sleep, then?" I asked.

"Out here?"

I shrugged. It was all an adventure, and I didn't really mind. What we didn't realize, though, was how much the fall temperatures of northern Nevada plummeted at night. John and I huddled together and woke up freezing cold, hungry, and staring up at the sight of a middle-aged woman who I assumed was John's former foster mom.

"There was a frost last night," she said. "You better come on in and warm up. I made you some breakfast."

She was a kind woman, but she had to let the authorities know that we were there, so while we ate, the police were called. My heart sank when I thought I was going back to Katie's, but I was quite pleased when a nice middle-aged police officer arrived and told John and me that instead we were going to juvenile hall—Wittenberg Hall to be specific—a secure holding facility for the temporary detention of juvenile offenders.

I'd heard of Wittenberg. Some of the older boys at school had mentioned it as a place where bad kids who'd gotten into one too many fights would be sent. Apparently, it was a pretty rough place where kids, especially newcomers like us, got beaten up on a regular basis and guards were unusually cruel. I didn't care about that. I wanted out from Katie's, and I would deal with whatever came next.

The police officer tasked with delivering John and me to this apparent hellhole didn't seem to think we posed a major threat so he let me ride up front with him. I watched the scenery pass by until just before midday when we pulled up to the front of a series of foreboding, plain brick buildings with the Sierra mountains looming in the distance behind them. My mind reeled with images of prison that I had seen on television, but then, as we walked through the entrance, we were met with the delicious smell of freshly baked bread and the face of a very friendly looking guard. Could this be the place everyone had spoken about? The guard looked at John and me in disbelief.

"What have you two young fellas done?" he asked.

"Runaways," said the police officer.

"Now, what would cause you to do a thing like that?" asked the guard.

"I'm sick of pulling weeds," I blurted out, as if this was perfectly reasonable.

The guard and the officer laughed and shook their heads. "You guys ran away because your foster parents wanted you to pull some weeds?" asked the guard. I nodded. It was obvious that these two seasoned veterans viewed John and me as mere children who did not yet realize how rough and tough the real world could be. In reality, John and I were all too aware of the harsh realities of life.

The guard checked us in, searching us for contraband. We had nothing on us, of course. Then he casually asked if we were hungry. "We got salad, mac and cheese, fresh bread, and ice-cold Coca Colas," he said. "Does that sound good?"

"Yes, please!" we said together.

The guard fetched us two trays of food. "You'll have to go to the tank to eat it," he said. "Follow me."

We nodded, picked up our trays, and headed down the hall where we entered a small room. Inside was an older teenage boy and as John and I sat down and started eating, he stared at us, looking tired and pissed off. The guard looked him straight in the eyes and said, "If you touch these kids, I will come back and beat the fuck out of you personally." I didn't flinch. I'd heard worse. I carried on eating.

CHAPTER SEVENTEEN

How could I have left them behind? Guilt tore at me as I thought about my siblings back at Katie's and Marjorie's. They were too young to run away. Weren't they? How far would John and I have gotten with them along for the ride? Probably not far. I rang Dana and explained as best I could. He seemed to understand.

I had always assumed that time spent in jail, even juvenile jail, would be dismal. However, Wittenberg provided me with some important insight and even some direction in my life. I was treated fairly and was able to eat as much as I liked. I even had my own room. Of course, it was a cell. But not to me. It was my room. I had my own space, and privacy, which I really appreciated.

During a typical day, I'd get up, brush my teeth, have breakfast, and then go to school inside the facility. I was placed in the fifth grade. After lunch, we'd go out to the yard and play hoops for an hour or so. Then more schoolwork. After dinner, we would watch TV for a couple of hours, then we'd go back to our cells and read books. It was great to have something to read other than the Bible.

At bedtime, there was no teddy bear to cuddle with and no one to tuck me in. Then again, I don't think I'd ever been tucked in and kissed goodnight. Still, I cried those first few nights at Wittenberg. I cried as I realized that this was my life and that someone giving me a kiss and telling me it was going to be OK was not going to happen for me.

Eventually, I found solace in interacting with the other guys, by learning to play chess and basketball. I also worked in the mess hall, where I learned to cook. I attended church with some of the other inmates. But best of all, I watched *Dukes of Hazzard* on TV and ate ice cream every single night. I also had access to the library and constantly brought books back to my cell. I found solace in reading and, even though I was imprisoned, as the days went on, I started to feel liberated.

I recently told some friends I'd been in juvie. Their teenage daughter was horrified and said, "Oh my god, you were in prison? That's awful." But it didn't seem like jail to me; it seemed like a path to a new life. I suppose prison is awful when you have a lot to lose, but what did I have to lose? Prison gave me what humans need to survive: safety, shelter, and food. I found comfort in my cell, in the routine, the TV, the ice cream, the books, the friends, the structure, and, most importantly, a sense that someone or something—in this case a state-run institution—cared enough about me to think about how I was going to spend my day-to-day life. Everything depends on your frame of reference for how good or bad something seems. Wittenberg was a great and new experience for me. And it was a simple fact that my life in juvie was far better than my life in foster care.

Katie viewed foster children as a source of revenue and treated us as a "profit center," a department with a budget that she needed to strictly keep. She saved money by providing us with a meager allotment of food and by having us work for her. Unfortunately, however, after a brief stay at Wittenberg, I was returned to Katie's house. It was good to see my brothers and sister, but as soon as I could, I ran away again. I was moving from the role of caretaker to wanting to take care of Stephen. Are kids selfish? Yes. It's natural. But I wanted to be in charge of my life.

"This time," my social worker, Debbie, told me when she collected me from the police station, "you're going to Carson City, to the NNCH—the Northern Nevada Children's Home." I didn't know what this meant. "And Stephen," she told me, "you realize, don't you? This is your last chance before you get sent to jail."

I nodded. I hoped that this would be a good change and a new beginning of sorts. It didn't cross my mind to ask what I might be sent to jail for. What would my crime have been? Wanting love and nurturing after years of shit and neglect?

* * *

I was to live at NNCH for nearly the next five years, until one month before my fifteenth birthday. I arrived as a ten-year-old ward of the state in someone else's clothes that were two sizes too big.

The Northern Nevada Children's Home was in Carson City, in a complex that included the Nevada Supreme Court, the state legislature, and other state offices. The home and its counterpart in southern Nevada had been created to give long-term foster children the chance to feel like they were part of a family. It was for girls and boys who had little chance of reuniting with their families. The building sat on fifteen acres of land right in the center of the capital city on a bustling main street. There was an outdoor tennis court, a basketball court, a bowling alley, a gym, and a recreation hall with pool tables, Ping-Pong tables, and assorted video games.

There were seven individual one-story homes that housed up to twelve children at a time and a commissary that provided supplies to the entire campus. Children were given a ten-dollar-per-month allowance. The home offered full medical services, tutoring services for children who fell behind on their grades, and counselors to support children who were suffering emotionally and/or psychologically. I was so stoic, keeping my feelings buried deep inside, that these services were never offered to me. In addition, the children in each home, or "cottage" as they were called, were taken on a special outing each year to places like Disneyland or other amusement parks, all funded by the state.

Despite the amenities, NNCH was still an institution. And it was the last stop before a child was sent to a long-term prison as a juvenile offender. The idea was to help those children who were heading in the wrong direction by offering them one last chance before sending them off to jail. To reinforce how high the stakes were, the Nevada maximum security prison was one mile down the road. The prison was a foreboding presence that cast a long shadow over NNCH.

Tom Hughes was the home's social worker. He was extremely nice and gave me background information including the fact that I'd be living in Cottage One with Barbara and Lee Wilhelm, the cottage parents.

"You'll call them Mom and Dad Wilhelm," he told me.

Whatever, I thought. "OK," I said.

Mom and Dad Wilhelm were off duty when I arrived, so a woman called "Mom Peggy" helped me check in and showed me around. Cottage One was warm and welcoming with wood-paneled walls. There were seven bedrooms for the children plus one bedroom for the house parents and another bedroom for the "relief" parents who came in on the house parents' day off. The home had a fairly large living room with two large bathrooms. When I began living there, Cottage One was occupied by ten boys ranging in age from one to seventeen years. I was shown to a room that had two single beds.

"Put your stuff away," Peggy told me. "Your bed is on the left."

I had a box of bits that I'd brought from Katie's. Just a few clothes, hand-me-downs that were either too big or too small, and a yo-yo I bought from my Bubbalicious money. I put them where I thought best.

That night, after I was introduced to my roommate, Richard, I got into bed and curled up on my side facing the wall. It was February and I was cold, despite the soft blowing of some sort of heating system. My mother came into my mind. Then Dana. Should I have called the front desk of the motel that day? Was that the right thing to do? Would we all still be together if I hadn't? Was Dana OK?

Our mother had abandoned us and now I had abandoned Dana. My brother. My best friend and the only person I could rely on. Tears rolled down my face and soaked into my pillow.

* * *

The next morning, I went to my new school and when I got home, Barbara, or "Mom Wilhelm," greeted me at the front door. A heavyset, nondescript woman in her midforties, Barbara had brown hair pulled back in a bun. She was wearing blue jeans and white tennis shoes and had a straightforward demeanor.

"Dad will be back here shortly and tell you what to do with your things," she told me.

Dad? OK. Bizarre, but whatever makes you happy, I thought.

She then explained various housekeeping rules. I listened politely and excused myself to go up to my room. I opened the door, intending to put my school bag away, but was shocked to see that all my things were strewn about the room and that my bed had been taken apart and my sheets and blankets had been thrown onto the floor. I turned around to find a man who I presumed to be Lee Wilhelm standing behind me with his hands on his hips.

"Hello, young man," he said. "Welcome to Cottage One. I am your cottage dad, Lee Wilhelm. First things first. You need to put your things away, and it needs to be done correctly."

Lee proceeded to demonstrate to me how to make my bed with hospital corners and how to fold my shirts and underwear. I was taken aback since I had not been told what to do by a man since my time with Gus. But it was clear that Lee was not someone to be messed around with, so I complied. Thin and tall, Lee had cropped hair, a full graying beard, and metal-rimmed glasses. I guessed he was a former military man, and I would soon discover that I was right. He wore a denim shirt and blue jeans with a thick belt to which was attached an enormous key ring that held a vast array of keys.

That night, and for many nights afterward, I continued to cry myself to sleep. The next day, I asked to call Dana.

"No contact with anyone for thirty days," Lee told me.

"Why?" I asked.

"Policy," he said.

Punishment. Again. And for what purpose?

And that was that. I already understood that my mother was not coming for me. And although I would eventually be able to speak to Dana on the telephone, I was alone, and I would have to get on with it. I had followed my own path and it had brought me to this children's home—a place where anyone could be called "Mom." With that title starting to mean less, I naturally started to refer to my own mother as Brenda.

As the days went on, I began to understand the routine of the home. Lee and Barbara worked Friday through Tuesday and then, on their days off, Peggy came to take care of the home. Lee was also in charge of the commissary and responsible for the ordering, unloading, and storing of the food for the seven cottages. He ran a tight ship and could be a tough disciplinarian. Lee possessed a black-and-white worldview and expected his charges to follow his rules exactly without deviation, engendering a great deal of anger in me. I hated being told that I had to put a napkin in my lap when I ate, or not to put my elbows on the table. Dave at La Casa had just been glad we were eating, Katie had allocated our food meagerly...but under Lee's mandate there was a strict timetable for even the smallest actions from when to eat, when to bathe, and when to go to bed. I felt as if I was seven years old again. Basically, it was bootcamp for kids.

In all fairness, Lee did not have an easy job as he had been tasked with trying to make men out of boys from all sides of the tracks, encompassing various racial, ethnic, and socioeconomic backgrounds, many of whom suffered from severe emotional and psychological problems. He was preparing us for the world. I didn't realize that at the time, of course. I just felt aggrieved and noted that even when I did follow all of Lee's rules to the letter, he rarely uttered any praise or acknowledged good behavior.

RENO
THE BIGGEST LITTLE CITY IN THE WORLD

Hotel Goodbyes

CHAPTER EIGHTEEN

The Kaniskys of *Gimme a Break*, the Huxtables of *The Cosby Show*, the Jacksons of *Diff'rent Strokes*, the Keatons of *Family Ties*, and the Evans of *Good Times*...

American television in the 1980s featured families of all kinds who stuck together through thick and thin. It was already crystal clear to me that I didn't have a family, but the point was being rammed home every time I turned on the TV. And it wasn't just on television. Every day when I arrived at school, I saw kids getting out of their cars, being kissed and hugged by their parents.

Each night I went to bed at 9:00 p.m. and lay there until 10:00 or 11:00 p.m., thinking about my life and the fact that I did not have what made people successful. I went to my friends' houses after school or to parties, sometimes staying over, and saw very clearly that I was not set up to be a success like my friends who had families. After basketball practice, their parents picked them up and they'd get in their cars. When we left our home, the Northern Nevada Children's Home, it was embarrassing. We had huge vans with "Official Use Only" written on the side. Not that I wanted a fancy car. I just wanted what my friends had. They had families who looked like them and talked like them; they had a shared history; they knew who their grandmother was, who their brothers were; their uncles lived down the street; their mother worked for the state; their dad was a teacher; their families were entirely ingrained into their lives. They didn't live with a group of kids who looked different from them and two days a week a different woman would come in and take care of the kids because the other people had to go off on break for two days. It wasn't about money either. Carson had people from all socioeconomic backgrounds, but even the people who were very poor still had a cohesive family for the most part.

It was going to take more than a Mom and Dad Wilhelm to form a family that meant something to me. They weren't attached to me or invested in me, and I felt nothing toward them. It was a functional, clinical relationship. The state knew it. Kids did OK in orphanages and children's homes, but if they could get kids adopted into homes, then quite often they would thrive.

The NNCH home had over seventy kids and we all went to different elementary, middle, and high schools. I attended Bordewich Bray Elementary. Once again, school was a haven for me, and I relished spending time with kids my age instead of being the loner I was when I lived with Brenda. I also enjoyed being away from my cottage parents. In many ways, I was just like any other sixth grader. But as soon as the other kids found I was from "the home," I stood out again, even though people were generally friendly and nice. The home had quite a reputation and the kids from the home were considered "bad." Many *were* bad, no argument, but only because they had been neglected or abused. I had experienced tremendous hardship and trauma, but my experiences paled in comparison to some of the others who had been beaten, abused, neglected, or raped. Some children's parents were addicts who had died. One was just a baby when his mother killed his abusive father. I never considered myself a victim and neither did most of the other kids, but their pain was plain to see on their faces. We were survivors. But like kids everywhere, the kids at the home were all dreamers. We wanted to be singers, dancers, and basketball players. We dreamed of having families of our own. We wanted to belong somewhere and not feel like guests.

Brenda was not on my mind in those early months as much as my siblings were. When I was finally allowed to, I called Dana.

"Dad came," he said.

I shuddered slightly at the thought of Gus.

"He took Brian, Eugene, and Tierra home with him."

"With Mom?" I asked.

"No, just him."

Anxiety sliced me. Dana had been left again. He was alone.

"When are we going to see each other again?" he asked me.

"I don't know," I said. "I guess we'll figure something out."

I liked spending my allowance at the mall, going to A&W Restaurants to drink root beer floats, or playing video games like Ms. Pac-Man. But when I knew Dana's birthday was coming up, I saved up my allowance and went to JC Penney to buy him a remote-controlled car. I then went to the Post Office to wrap and send it. I'm not sure if he ever received the gift. Sometime later, I learned, Marjorie had sent Dana to Pacific Union College Prep School in Napa Valley, California. Despite this, and our young ages, we managed to keep in touch.

Several months after I arrived at NNCH, John Kinsey, my former housemate at Katie's, arrived and moved into Cottage Six—the one next to mine. It was good to see him again and we started hanging out. Over time, people began comparing us to each other. John was Black; I was Black. He lived at the home; I lived at the home. When folks saw me, they'd ask, "Where's Kinsey?" as if we were twins. We looked nothing alike, but because we had similar backgrounds and histories, folks assumed we were always together and close friends. John and I attended different schools for junior high most likely because the home, I believe, wanted to separate us from each other and allow us to be exposed to other students.

An old mining town, Carson City retained the feel of a typical Western town with its honky-tonk architecture, wide main street, and hot, dry climate. When I moved to Carson in the early 1980s, the town enjoyed a strong economy based on state funding. Most of the population was Caucasian with a small but significant Native American population residing on the nearby reservation. There were also a small number of Mexican immigrants and African Americans.

Nevada has traditionally been a gaming and mining state, but it is misleading to say that gaming, alcohol sales, and prostitution are beneficial to a state's economy as studies demonstrate that states with a large presence of such vices tend to have much higher rates of crime and substance abuse. Many of the children who were placed in NNCH were there because members of their families had gotten caught up in some of the many vices that proliferated in the area.

Many of the youth in the Carson community were involved in drugs, and the home was littered with kids who used and sold: getting high to numb the trauma that had marred their young lives. Drugs were everywhere, and it would have been easy for me to get involved.

But having witnessed firsthand the havoc that drug and alcohol abuse inflicts on people, I had no desire to partake.

It didn't take me too long to figure out that there were two types of kids who succeeded in Carson City: smart kids and athletes. The "Heshers," with their long hair and penchant for heavy metal music and marijuana were the other extreme. I had no issues with them; I just wasn't into drugs. At that time, the most famous athletes from Carson City were Matt Williams, Charlie Kerfeld, and Bob Ayrault. They were talented and popular baseball players and I reckoned that I would have to get involved with sports to stay on the straight and narrow, which is how, after seventh grade, I came to spend my summer on the basketball court.

The home had both an outdoor basketball court and an old gymnasium that had been converted into a basketball court in the late 1970s. In order to use the old gym, you had to be accompanied by an adult. Cottage dads didn't really play with us kids, so I was relegated to the outdoor court.

Every day I got out onto the court in the ferocious Nevada sun and steered clear of the kids who were involved in drugs. Kids who had befriended youngsters from outside the home often invited them in to use the facilities, so all summer there were opportunities to meet people, including girls, from outside NNCH.

What I liked best about sports was the feeling of honing a craft. Since I was too young to get a job, I would stay on the court for hours just practicing my shots. Sometimes other kids would join me, but I spent a lot of time by myself on that hot asphalt.

One of the unique things about the home was that it was extremely close to the state buildings and the state capitol was literally across the street. One day I was busy rebounding my shot on the outdoor court when a man came over and said, "Hey there. Wanna come play with us inside where it's nice and cool? We need an extra player to even out the teams."

I was reluctant at first because I wasn't sure if I was allowed, but I told him, "Sure." It was fantastic. It wasn't that I was that good at basketball—quite the opposite in fact—but the older guys were fine with that because I would run hard and pass them the ball and try to get rebounds. It felt great to play hoops with other people, especially men much older than myself. I guess they were some of my first positive male role models.

I played with them many times afterward until, one day, Lee told me I couldn't. He never gave a reason why and I think he just didn't like the fact that I was engaging in an activity outside of his control. Luckily, Mr. Alder, the home administrator who played with the guys, overruled him and whenever those guys needed an extra person to play, they called on me. I ended up playing with them for many years to come, and it was years before I realized I had been playing with state administrators and even with the future governor of Nevada himself, Bob Miller.

CHAPTER NINETEEN

"*I* am going to kill her."

My cottage brothers looked up from their homework. "I mean it," I said.

I had been living at the Northern Nevada Children's Home for a year and a half. Every night after dinner, those of us that had homework sat together to complete it. This night was no different, but my mind wasn't on my schoolwork. I'd had enough.

When I first moved into NNCH, it was clear that I was not going to be like the other kids in the home. I distanced myself from most people and spent most of my time alone shooting hoops. I didn't smile at adults or show any signs of enjoyment, but neither did I flip out like other kids or talk back to Lee or Barbara. I was compliant. I was determined not to showcase my pain like the other kids. But as time went on, I felt I had to control my own destiny. I started not asking for permission. If I needed to stay behind at school to speak to a teacher, I would do it. If the cottage was going to one church, I would choose to go to a different one.

So, I had a plan. And the "her" I was referring to was Mom Wilhelm.

Barbara was pleasant, but distant. I don't remember what she had done to anger me so much. Was it Brenda I actually wanted to hurt, and I was just lashing out on the closest thing I had to a mother figure at the time? Maybe. Or maybe Barbara had done something any adult would do to a twelve-year-old child. However, I did not consider myself a child anymore and whatever it was, it was enough for me to want to kill Barbara. I knew that Barbara was a diabetic, and I thought that she needed to take insulin and could not eat sugar. As it was summer, Barbara always enjoyed a glass of iced tea with dinner and I came up with a plan to dump a pile of sugar in her iced tea, thereby killing her. It was a childishly simple solution to my problem.

The next night before dinner, I made sure there was enough sugar in the sugar bowl and at 6:00 p.m., we boys gathered together as normal. It was my turn to serve the drinks and I dutifully filled the glasses according to each person's preference. As usual, Barbara requested iced tea. I filled her glass and as she turned to help feed Charlie, who was still in a high chair, I quickly stirred two heaping spoonfuls of sugar into the tea and carefully placed it next to her dinner plate. All the other boys had seen what I had done, but I didn't care. I casually sat down to eat my dinner and prepared to watch the entire thing go down. Barbara finished giving Charlie his mouthful of mashed potato, wiped his chin, and picked up her glass of iced tea.

"Wait, Mom. Don't drink it. Stop!"

It was Joe, a much older kid of about sixteen, who had yelled the warning.

"What are you talking about?" asked Barbara.

"Steve put sugar in your glass," Joe continued. "I saw him do it. He wanted to kill you."

Any sense that I was in control of the situation quickly faded. Barbara kept her cool.

"Please leave the table, Stephen," she said.

I complied and walked slowly to my room, my heart heavy with the anticipation of the punishment that awaited. Barbara's reaction was not what I expected and now I had no idea what I was going to face. As it turned out, I wasn't allowed to play outside and had to do all the dishes for a month. More significant was a conversation I had with Lee the following day.

"Stephen," he began, having taken me into the garden. "You're a good kid, but you need to act like a kid and stop acting like an adult. You should be a kid while you still have the time."

His words hit home. He had noticed something that other adults had not. I was acting like an adult. Being a child made me vulnerable. I'd never had an adult to rely on, so I had become my own grown-up. And as the caregiver to my siblings, I had learned how to make practical decisions as quickly as possible. It was hard for me to just have fun and be a kid. It was a hard concept for a kid to grasp, but Lee knew I would understand. His words sunk deep into my soul, and I decided that despite what I had endured, I would take a fresh perspective on life.

The next day I found Barbara sitting in the kitchen reading a newspaper and drinking coffee. I walked toward her and quietly said, "I'm sorry."

"For what?" she asked.

"For putting sugar in your iced tea and trying to kill you," I stammered.

The words sounded stupid, and I realized how stupid I had been. Barbara nodded and went back to her newspaper. She didn't talk to me for about a month, but after that, she began to be extremely kind to me. Barbara wasn't my mom, but she became mom-like. I really appreciated that she developed a special and meaningful relationship with me, where we chatted with each other. She took an interest in my plans, simple things such as when I was trying out for the basketball team. When I was looking for a summer job, I asked her what she'd done when she was young. It was new to me to engage with other people in that manner and it felt good.

CHAPTER TWENTY

Lift your head up high and scream out to the world 'I know I am someone,' and let the truth unfurl / No one can hurt you now because you know what's true / Yes, I believe in me, so do believe in you.
—MICHAEL JACKSON, "WANNA BE
STARTIN' SOMETHIN'"

*T*he *Cosby Show* made me want to be a lawyer or a US senator. Brenda had always been very political, so I guess it was in my bones. But before I could become a lawyer or a senator, I had to follow Lee's advice and become just a kid. His words had really gone to my core and when I looked for joy, I found Bill Burks, another Black kid in the home. Even though he was a couple of years older than me, Bill seemed to know all about being a kid. On summer days when not much was happening, Bill would stand up in front of a group of about thirty of us and begin telling hilarious stories punctuated by song and dance routines—all performed with perfect comic timing. He'd then ask if anyone else wanted to perform. I started going out to watch Bill's comedy routines and it felt great to be there with everyone else, busting up laughing for what felt like hours on end. It's such a skill to make people laugh like that, and Bill is one of the funniest people I have ever met. And it's powerful, a really good way of connecting. I liked Bill—always wearing a big smile—and he liked something in me too. We became great friends and, since he was really popular around town, he introduced me to a lot of people.

The 1980s were Michael Jackson's era, and the breakdance craze of popping and breaking, which came from the New York City street dance movement, was massive. We couldn't get enough of it, especially after we had a group of about ten Black guys come and perform for us at NNCH. To see this kind of dancing live was mind-blowing. It made it real, and I could see it was something I could learn to do. It came reasonably naturally to me, but I could see that it required a lot of practice to become good. It also required showmanship and passion. I had both and spent hours working on my moves in the cottage bathroom, where there was a large mirror. I would take my little tape recorder in and play the song "Egyptian Lover" or other rap songs. Sometimes kids asked to join me in the bathroom to watch me practice—other times they told me to get the hell out. I never did.

There were loads of kids in Carson who loved to breakdance, but I would say John Kinsey was the best breaker and I was the best popper. Bill Burks was kind of the showman, telling jokes and introducing the acts. One time, when Bill invited people up to perform, the others asked to see my moves, so I got up and showed them. It felt great and before long, Kinsey and Bill found a boom box sound system and we'd go around town to have a pop-off, a breakdance competition, wherever we could find the space—even in the lobby of the local skating rink. Bill moved out of the home just as Kinsey and I were getting good at this stuff, so two new kids joined our dance troupe, Billy Lightfoot and Rich Aguilera. The four of us got so good that we were asked to perform at high school dances. In 1984, the local movie theater showed two films about breakdancing, *Beat Street* and *Breaking*. The movie theaters asked several of us to come to the opening night of the two movies so that we could dance before the film came on. Both events were packed with hundreds of people screaming and cheering. We became pretty popular around Carson because of those events.

Then, we decided that we wanted to be rappers. We'd sing in the school assemblies and later in high school, I wrote rap songs for our football team. One song was called "Senators," since our mascot was a senator because Carson was the state capital. Kinsey would beatbox while Travis Hopper and I performed the song. Travis was a white kid from our high school who was hilarious, and his dad, my baseball coach, was a great guy. For the first time, I started to enjoy being a kid .

* * *

One of the perks that the kids at the home enjoyed was the chance to take trips in the summer. The Wilhelms decided to let us kids figure out where we were going to go. We settled on Seattle as our destination. Then, we began the process of plotting our course to the Pacific Northwest. The Wilhelms were outdoor folks, so we would be camping along the way near Mount Rainier and along the Oregon coast, ending up at the famous Space Needle.

This was the first vacation and camping trip I had ever been on in my life. Everyone was excited and I was no exception. As we drove through the Northern Sierras and continued on through California, passing the majestic Mount Shasta and other natural wonders, I sat in the back of the van and marveled at the incredible scenery. It's hard to put into words how much this experience nurtured my soul. For the first time in my life, I was able to slow down, sit still, and just watch the world go by.

Unlike my many previous Greyhound bus trips, I wasn't overwhelmed with worry or concern about what lay ahead or where this adventure would take me. We had a plan, and I was confident knowing where we were going. I did not have to worry about what kind of obstacles I would face after such a long trip and, as a result, I could simply enjoy myself.

Highway 5, which is the main north-south highway, took us through California, Oregon, and Washington. Our trip lasted about ten days. The first night we camped at the foot of Mount Shasta and eventually arrived outside Seattle. We spent five days touring in and around the Seattle area. We went to one of the neighboring islands, camped and fished near Mount Rainier, and visited a reservation, where we watched a Native American ceremony and ate a delicious salmon meal. We also visited various sites in the city itself, culminating in a trip to the Space Needle. Decades later, I would end up working at Amazon there, with my team office being right there in the heart of Seattle.

One of the highlights was a trip to the Kingdome stadium to see the Oakland A's play baseball. That year, 1984, was the final season of Rickey Henderson's first stint with the Oakland A's. He had started to develop more of a power stroke, hitting sixteen home runs while leading the league in stolen bases (66), finishing second in runs scored (113) and third in on-base percentage. We met him after the game and got his autograph, which was awesome.

On the way back to Nevada, we stopped in Portland, Oregon, then camped for a few days in Coos Bay. I was awestruck by the juxtaposition of the deep green forest, sandy coastline, and plunging sea cliffs. The campsite was great fun as it was filled with many other groups of kids our age. One night, several of my friends from the home—Steve, Jeff, and Dave—gathered together in my tent. When bedtime came, we heard Dad Wilhelm's voice call out, "Good NIGHT, gentlemen!" I had just finished telling some crazy ghost story I'd made up. Steve was a kid known for getting into trouble and his crazy antics often led to Dad Wilhelm saying, "Barbara, write him up!" It was not unusual to get "written up" by Lee, and we were never quite sure of what the consequences would be, nor did we care. Steve chose this perfect moment to say loudly in a baby voice, "Hey, Daddy Wilhelm, what's a muff?"

"Barbara, write him up!" roared Lee from right outside the tent.

The whole tent erupted in laughter, and we didn't stop laughing until dawn. Many years have passed, and we still laugh about it today when we get together.

Those were happy days. We swam in the bay, explored the forest, and caught live crab for our dinner. By the end of the trip, I had a better appreciation for the Wilhelms as parents and for Lee, in particular.

At NNCH, we all had to attend Lutheran church, which was pretty conservative. I liked church, but decided to find one that suited me better—a Baptist church with great music—across the road from the Lutheran church. Lee and Barbara felt the Baptist church was too fun, with its teen-targeted events such as youth lock-ins, but I still went.

The Baptist church organized an annual trip to Great America, a theme park in the California Bay Area. The church would hire a bus and take about sixty kids. It cost thirty dollars each, which was a lot of money back then. When the time came for me to go on the trip, I had saved up thirty dollars from my monthly allowance, but I asked the Wilhelms if I would get extra money for anything else I might need on the trip, such as food, which I'd been told would cost about ten dollars. Being characteristically strict, the Wilhelms recommended I pack a lunch instead. Clearly, they had never walked around a theme park and had the sweet smell of french fries call to their souls.

When I arrived at the church and boarded the bus, I was informed that the cost was now forty dollars. I was stunned and told Brian, the youth leader, that I didn't have that much with me. "Do you have any spending money for the trip? Maybe you could use that?" he asked.

"I don't," I said, looking at my sneakers. "Thirty dollars is all I have."

"OK," he said. "That's OK. We'll figure it out."

I stood there, holding my lunch bag and fidgeting with the zipper on my sweatshirt. *I shouldn't be here.* What made me think I was like other people and could afford such a trip? I was mad at my cottage parents. I'd never been to a theme park but surely, they knew what this stuff cost.

Brian nodded to me, saying, "Come on, Steve. Why don't you take a seat over there next to Theresa Davis." She was an older girl, very nice, and I knew her younger sister, Samee. I slowly took my seat next to her, sliding my lunch bag under the seat in front of me. Once everyone else was seated, the bus driver took his seat, adjusted his rearview mirror, and pulled out onto the highway. The kids were really nice to me, and we chatted and laughed during the long ride to the Bay Area.

Just before we arrived at Great America, Brian walked down the aisle and addressed the kids. "Now, you all know that this trip is an opportunity for you to have a little fun and enjoy yourselves. But it is also an opportunity for you to demonstrate compassion for one another," he began. "There is a member of our group who does not have enough money for our trip. I am asking you now to think about the model that Jesus has provided to us and consider sparing a few dollars for Steve."

Out of the corner of my eye, I saw kids rooting around in their pockets and rifling through their bags for dollar bills and spare change. I was overcome with both gratitude and embarrassment as they walked by me to get off the bus, with each one passing me money. Two dollars. Five dollars. Ten dollars. The money kept on coming. I was grateful and deeply humbled. These were kids from regular families who didn't have loads of money.

In the end, I had enough money to buy a soft drink, hot food, and some other goodies. I bought photos from the rides and went into a recording studio they had there. For fifteen dollars, you could record a song on a cassette. I recorded Kool and The Gang's "Cherish the Love" and Lionel Richie's "Hello." It was such a cool experience to step in a studio and feel like a star.

Back on the bus, someone asked to play it through the speakers so that everyone could hear it. I was embarrassed but agreed. That day stands out in my mind as one of the best trips of my life. It was one of the few times in my life where I felt like a carefree kid with nothing to worry about.

RENO

THE BIGGEST LITTLE CITY IN THE WORLD

Hotel Goodbyes

CHAPTER TWENTY-ONE

How the hell am I going to get into college if I am in a special education class?

It was September 1984, and I was almost thirteen years old. I was leaving Bordewich Bray Elementary to start the seventh grade at Eagle Valley Junior High. In sixth grade, I was so advanced in math that I regularly finished my work early and ended up playing chess with my teacher, Mr. Kremers. But I struggled with English, which meant that according to my official record, I was considered to be "learning disabled." Therefore, at the beginning of seventh grade, I was put into special ed classes for English. At first, I wasn't upset as it meant I could get extra help from some great teachers. However, I was soon surrounded by students who were significantly less advanced than I was.

I wanted to be with my friends. Plus, in two years I would be going into my freshman year in high school and needed good grades to be able to play football. But most importantly, I thought that if I remained in special ed classes, I wouldn't get to college and become a politician. School was my sanctuary and, despite my struggles, it was where I needed to be to build my future. I knew that. However, I could see that the school had no intention of taking me out of special ed classes and NNCH wasn't going to do anything about it either. So, in the eighth grade, I forged the necessary signatures of my teachers, my social workers, and even Lee Wilhelm, stating that I should be put into regular classes like all the other students. The school did not recognize my handwriting, so my request was approved, and I was immediately moved to a regular class just in time to head into ninth grade.

At that time in Carson, ninth graders did not attend high school, but remained at their local middle school with the seventh and eighth graders. This became problematic if you were a member of one of the high school sports teams as you had to take a bus over to the high school for practice. It was complicated but worth it as it did facilitate important relationships and connections between the kids who attended different middle schools. During ninth grade, my freshman year, when I was fourteen years old, we had joint football, baseball, and track teams at the high school, but an independent basketball team at the middle school.

I played freshman football at the high school, basketball at the junior high school, and because I was not a very good baseball player, I ended up running track at the high school instead. I participated in all kinds of events including the 100-meter dash, the open 400-meter event, the shot put, and the high jump. The best part about running track was that it enabled me to get to know some of the older high school students, from whom I gleaned some important advice, not just about track and field but about life in general.

Although I was a freshman, there were several seniors and juniors on our track team. Some of the senior boys also played football like Andy Sharp, Tony Smiderle, Mickey Quilici, Andy Goldsmith, Fred Radtke, Anthony Vollet, and Jim Reid, so I knew them pretty well from playing football in the fall. I started to hang out with the seniors during practice and ended up becoming good friends with many of these guys.

One of them, Frank "The Tank" Granier, took an interest in me. Frank was the starting running back on the football team and a very popular guy. His father was a history teacher at the school. One day, as we were sitting on the grass and stretching after practice, Frank said something that had a profound impact and got me thinking in important ways about how others perceived me.

"Steve. You know, you're a really nice guy," Frank began. "But you never smile. I mean, you've always got this mean, tough look on your face."

Frank proceeded to explain to me that no matter how nice I was, my grimace made me appear unfriendly and unapproachable. He got me to practice smiling for a few minutes. From then on, I made a special effort to smile more. It may seem like a simple observation, but Frank's remark resonated with me. I am sure Frank had no comprehension of what I had been through and why I did not smile much. But he was right. At that point in my life, I had things to smile about, unlike my early years. I had a stable home environment with lots of friends. I was playing sports competitively and enjoying school. His simple observation was a major turning point for me. From that point on, I slowly began to shed some of the weight of my troubled past. I began to comprehend how much better my life had become and how much more there was for me to achieve.

RENO

THE BIGGEST LITTLE CITY IN THE WORLD

Hotel Goodbyes

CHAPTER TWENTY-TWO

*S*ome folks grow up in a great family. Plenty of others grow up in a family where they don't spend time with their relatives except on holidays or at family reunions. But that's still a family. Those folks have people who look like them. They have people who sound like them. They have siblings with shared experiences—both good and bad.

Folks from these families generally succeed. They have a great foundation upon which to build their lives. But sometimes, kids don't appreciate what they have.

"Oh my God, my mom is driving me crazy."

"My dad, man. What a jerk."

"I can't wait to get out of this house."

My friends were normal teenagers. And they complained about their parents. A lot. Eventually, I had to say something.

"Your parents are making you do your homework? Is that bad? You have a house. You guys are doing stuff. You have a family that cares about you. How bad can it be?"

I know that all kids complain about their parents, how they don't understand them, how they don't like their music, how they say they smell funny, which kids do. But I would challenge them when they said crazy stuff like "We're not rich."

"Oh, you're not rich? You've got food in the refrigerator!" I would say.

I had friends whose parents were dentists, or their family owned a law office or an appliance store, and they'd moan about not having enough. "OK, but you still have nice shit," I'd tell them. "This is good, dude. What's the problem here? You've got a pool! It's sweet. This looks pretty good to me!"

I understood why my friends didn't always appreciate their parents, but it was sometimes hard to hear for someone like me, who had no parents at all.

As I turned fourteen, I started to see my friends leave the home and move in with families who had adopted them—first Bill Burks, then Steve Alexander, then John Kinsey, and finally Dave Culjis. I use the term "adopted" loosely because it's rare for an older child, like a teenager, to be legally adopted by their host family. But "adopted" is the phrase we always used, because it's a family inviting you to come live with them. This is very different from having the state place you in a foster home among total strangers.

It was painful to see my friends leave the home to be adopted by new families. I knew deep in my bones that there was more for me than simply living at NNCH. I desperately wanted to be with a family. I was in awe of the fact that most parents cared for and dedicated their lives to raising their children. My friends outside the home simply did not realize how lucky they were to have grown up in warm, loving, stable families.

I was popular in school, and my friends loved inviting me over to their homes, like the Tella or Kenoyer families. They were nervous at first because I could be quite brash and loud at school. I loved to make my friends laugh, and I would say anything to achieve that, no matter how outrageous. A lot of kids from the home were like that. Maybe it was a release. Who knows. A lot of comedy comes from pain. However, friends were not aware of my ability to judge an appropriate audience. I was also able to build relationships with a wide mix of people very quickly, not that I fully recognized this at the time. When my friends invited me over to their homes to meet their parents, many of them were surprised at how polite I was. Almost all of them commented on how impressed they were with my ability to interact successfully with their parents. Many of my friends would tell me later that their parents really enjoyed meeting me. If they heard me telling their children how lucky they were to have such loving parents, they appreciated that too.

I guess my friends anticipated that I would act wild like I sometimes did at school. What my friends didn't know was that I had spent nearly all my time with adults in my early years. I hadn't gone to swimming club or wrestling practice, and I hadn't stayed in any one place long enough to make friends and play outside with the kids on my block. For most of my young life, I only knew how to be around adults and how to take care of my siblings.

Bill Burks was one of my first close friends to be adopted and leave the home. One summer, Bill worked as a batboy for the Reno Padres, a Minor League Baseball team. The local newspaper ran an article on him, and as a result, a wealthier, white family from Reno came forward to adopt him. They moved him to a more affluent school near their home in the suburbs of Reno and even changed his name, which Lee Wilhelm thought was a terrible idea. I kept in touch with Bill after he left and was happily envious to go and visit him in his incredible new six-bedroom house. It certainly seemed as if Bill had it all, but as an impoverished, young Black boy, it was glaringly obvious that he was out of place with the families and friends in that community. It made me wonder if I would want to lose my identity to find a new family and home. Would I have to lose parts of myself to be accepted?

I lost touch with Bill eventually, but some years ago, I found out that, after an incident with the family, he was kicked out of his adoptive home. He then spent most of his adult life in and out of prison and is now homeless. It seemed that Bill simply wasn't prepared for life in such a drastically different environment. When he left NNCH and his high school, he was effectively removed from all his friends, mentors, and adults who knew where he had come from and who he was.

Steve Alexander had arrived at the home just a few weeks after I did, along with his sister. He was white, of Greek heritage, and when his father died there was no one to take care of him. "Crazy Steve" was wild. He never got into drugs or smoked, but he craved attention and was really into girls. When Steve departed, he moved in with the family of a high school friend of ours, Matt Wilkerson. But Steve also struggled in his new adoptive home, largely due to his deep-seated resistance to authority, characteristic of most of the children that lived in the home who wanted to be in control of their own lives. When Steve moved out of NNCH, I went to stay with him some weekends at the Wilkersons' and was horrified by his disrespectful behavior to his adoptive parents. It made me uncomfortable and when I challenged him, he would tell me that his foster mother didn't care about him. Steve resented his foster mom's relationship with her birth children. I think he was still struggling with losing his father at such a young age and not having a mother to take care of him. He started getting into a lot of trouble, and eventually his foster parents kicked him out.

When John Kinsey moved out, we kept in touch and graduated from high school together. A year later, he joined the military but had a short career before, like so many other foster children, becoming homeless. So, as well as seeing my cottage brothers be adopted, I also witnessed their struggles. It was hard for them to adapt, sometimes because of what they'd experienced. They were traumatized and their behavior was communicating that. Sometimes the foster families failed them. But it's not easy to adopt teenage boys, some of whom have been abused and have developed complex survival skills. I could see that. It was clear that I needed to be ever mindful to avoid making those same mistakes if and when the time came for me to move into a foster family of my own.

Despite those examples, I never lost my faith in the power of families. The overwhelming desire of the foster child—to be in control of his or her life, which had previously been at the mercy of the capricious whims of unstable adults—often morphed into a stubbornness that, in many cases, led to grave mistakes. I watched other kids struggle to adapt to the rules of their new households and grapple with the inevitable jealousy between the foster children and biological children. I kept this in mind if I was ever adopted.

Now that I have my own kids, and realize the challenges of delivering advice to young people, I can see that I was unusually good at accepting feedback about myself when I was younger. When important figures spoke to me about my demeanor and behavior, I was receptive and willing to adapt. I needed guidance and I knew this instinctively, so I listened. On some level, I knew that feedback was an expression of love, or at the very least, care. Was some of the feedback wrong? Of course, but I appreciated it as I tried to work out what to follow and what to ignore.

It hit me hard when another friend from the home, Dave Culjis, departed. We'd shared a room in the cottage and would lay on our beds, surrounded by Van Halen posters, listening to music, and chatting about girls. He was white, had long hair, played the electric guitar, and attended Carson Junior High—a different school from mine—so each night we would share what had happened during the day. Our close friendship continued into high school.

"Hey, man," he said, one night. "I'm leaving. The Walldeimisters have asked me to come live with them."

My heart skipped a beat. Someone else was leaving?

"Wow," I said. "That's awesome."

"Yeah, I'm pretty excited."

"I bet. What do you think it will be like?"

"Cool, I hope. Will you come and stay?"

"Sure. And I'll see you at church."

I was happy for Dave. Was I sad for myself? I think I was more reflective. People were hitting the road. I hoped I'd be next.

CHAPTER TWENTY-THREE

One of the few advantages of living at the home is that we were allowed to get jobs with the state government. Children who lived in the home were allowed to work from the age of fourteen to encourage them to earn their own money and gain experience, which would help them build a life when they left NNCH.

Since it was illegal for children under sixteen to work in the state of Nevada, NNCH successfully lobbied the state legislature for an exception and for funding to provide us summer jobs within various state departments. With the funding, the state established a nonprofit entity to provide not just employment but also job training and education, aided by additional federal matching funds. Prior to beginning one of these jobs, an eligible child was required to participate in a six-week training program, which covered all the job basics from filling out a job application to understanding the interview process to interviewing strategies. They even gave us tips about how to negotiate salaries. At the end of the class, we were each interviewed on camera so we could assess our presentation skills. Years later this remains one of the most important job trainings I have ever attended.

The first summer, I worked at the Army National Guard as a receptionist clerk and the following summer, I worked for the procurement outreach program where I was a clerk in the Nevada Budget Office.

Because of my work for the state government, I was later invited to provide testimony to the Nevada state legislature regarding whether the state should grant driver's licenses to foster children. The crux of the issue was who would be held responsible if one of these children got into a car accident. Foster children were considered wards of the state. The potential financial liability underlying this endeavor drew the attention of the state legislature. This issue also would have a potentially significant effect on foster children since if they were not allowed to obtain a driver's license at the age of sixteen, like most children, they would have to wait until they were eighteen. I was asked to come and testify before the Child and Protective Services committee.

I don't know how the committee chose me, especially because I was only fifteen years old, not even old enough to have a driver's license yet, but it was a terrific opportunity to participate in local government and make my voice heard, along with those of my fellow foster children, whom I felt I was representing. I was thrilled. As I entered the chambers and was brought before the committee, I was introduced to all its members, one of whom was Joe Neal, a state senator from Las Vegas. At the time, Neal was the only sitting African American state senator in the Nevada legislature. He represented a predominantly Black and Latino senate district just north of Las Vegas. He was also the chairman of the health and government affairs committees. Senator Neal was very well known for not taking any crap from anyone, and he only left the state senate many years later when term limits were introduced. I was nervous, but excited to address the committee and give my opinion on the issue of driver's licenses for foster children.

Once I began my testimony, the committee inquired, "Mr. Thompson, how would granting you, a foster child, a driver's license when you become sixteen make a difference in your life?"

"Well, it would help young students and foster kids get around the community more easily," I began. "It would also help them find jobs as they would be able to drive to places other than those they could walk to. As many of you know, we do not have a city bus system in Carson and neither do the rural areas of Nevada."

I gave my best shot at making the case for foster kids to have driver's licenses when other kids could get them, and after my testimony, I was asked to join Senator Neal for a meeting. He was very nice and chatty as he took me back to his chambers where he asked me to take a seat. Originally from Louisiana, Neal was a graduate of Southern University with a degree in political science and history. He went on to spend over twenty-five years in administration at the Reynolds Electrical and Engineering Company, while serving in the state senate.

"How many Black kids are there at your school?" he asked politely.

"Not many," I shrugged, wondering what was coming next.

"Look, son," Senator Neal continued. "I need to tell you that this town and your school just isn't made for you."

"What are you trying to say?" I asked.

"Carson City is a great community with some really good folks, but this just ain't a place for someone who looks like you do. It's not a place designed for young Black men to succeed," he said.

I didn't know what to say. This was the first time anyone had addressed the issue of race with me so openly. Of course, I was aware that I was one of only a handful of students of color at my school. But I had never seen it as any sort of hindrance. In fact, I rarely felt that anyone singled me out or treated me differently because I was Black. I said as much to the senator.

"C'mon, Steve," he said. "You're Black and this town was built for white people. I'm not trying to discourage you. I simply want you to be aware of the many challenges that you will have to face in order to succeed in this kind of environment."

As much as I appreciated his willingness to speak with me, I must admit that I was a bit confused and turned off by his remarks. I had never dwelled too much on my racial background. It wasn't until later in my life that I realized how right the senator was. But as a kid, what could I do? No one was coming to get me and drop me in Philly or south-central Los Angeles where there were more people who looked like me. I have always refused to allow myself to be defined or limited by my race. I have never been a fan of labels. Growing up as an adolescent in a predominantly white town, I had to move past my race in order to survive and to thrive.

I can honestly say that I never felt that I was perceived as a threat by people in my town, most likely due to the fact that there were so few Black people that the community saw us more as an anomaly rather than a danger. Many years later, I would understand that there is a huge difference between being a cute Black kid, who people sometimes called "Theo Huxtable" from the *Cosby Show*, and being a fully grown Black man in the United States. But my life has been nothing if not full of transitions.

In Carson City, I was unique in terms of being one of only a few African Americans in town. It wasn't a perfect community. At times, I got teased for the way I looked, and, on occasion, people told me frankly that they did not like me due to my skin color. Sometimes someone would roll down a car window and shout something offensive. However, those who did not like me based simply on my race were relatively few and I never understood that it might be part of some larger system of discrimination. Maybe if I'd grown up in an urban environment like Oakland, where the population was 70 percent Black at the time, I might have felt more tension between Black and white people. However, Carson was a small town, and I was not a threat to the established structure. Besides, I already possessed very clear vulnerabilities by virtue of my position as a foster child and a ward of the state. But Senator Neal's words always stayed with me.

RENO
THE BIGGEST LITTLE CITY IN THE WORLD

Hotel Goodbyes

CHAPTER TWENTY-FOUR

When "Crazy" Steve Alexander was living with the Wilkersons, I would often go over there to hang out with him and Matt Wilkerson. They lived right behind Gina Lopez, a girl from our school who was extremely friendly and popular. Everyone liked Gina. Somewhat petite, she was a terrific dancer and champion baton twirler. She and I had known each other since sixth grade and had taken seventh grade science together. I remember this class vividly because Gina sat two rows over from me and she missed an entire month of school that year. I later found out that it was because her father had died.

One day, Steve, Matt, and I went over to Gina's house and her mom, Kathy Lopez, opened the door.

"Oh, you must be the dancer that I've heard so much about!" she said to me. "Gina has told me all about you."

"Yes," I stammered.

"Wonderful!" She went on, "Would you dance for me? Show me some of your moves?"

I was embarrassed, so I mumbled, "Maybe later," and quickly departed.

But over time, I became more comfortable and began spending a lot of time at the Lopez residence with Gina and her mom, Kathy, who was very informal and treated us like adults. One day, when we got chatting, Kathy asked me if I wanted to work in her office in the health facilities department that summer. This department was responsible for monitoring and licensing all the senior living homes in the state of Nevada. Kathy was responsible for the inspectors, ensuring that they were accurately reporting the condition of the facilities and the health of the senior citizens who lived in them.

I had visited one of these senior homes once to sing Christmas carols to residents with my Baptist church. It had left quite an impression on me. An elderly woman was the first person I saw as we lined up to enter the facility. She sat crying in her wheelchair and tried to grab my hand as I walked in with the other kids. Unfortunately, I had to keep moving forward, outside of her grasp. Next, we started walking down the hallway and I looked to my left and saw a balding, elderly man in a wheelchair slumped to the side with an oxygen tank by his leg. He was gasping for air. I felt so sad at the sight of these disabled seniors sitting in the hallway. It was obvious to me that these folks were unattended and uncared for. We arrived at the room where we were performing and started to sing, squeezing together as if we were trying to insulate ourselves from the neglect in front of our eyes. As we began to sing "Silent Night" and other holiday favorites, the true meaning of the songs started to sink in. Not the meaning of Jesus and his birth, but the notion of caring for others. We sang several songs, and I felt every single word, moved by thoughts of how lucky I was.

As we walked, one of the older boys, Mike Stanley, was stopped by an old woman who pulled him close and whispered in his ear. I don't know what she said but as I looked around at the other kids, I noticed that most of them were crying. I know I was. I have rarely witnessed such misery before or since. These people wanted to be spoken to and touched but instead they had been reduced to commodities that someone was paid to take care of. We boarded the bus and rode home in silence.

Because of this experience, when Kathy asked me if I wanted to work with her in the health facilities department, I had a very clear sense of the kind of work that the inspectors were engaged in. I agreed but said I wouldn't be able to visit the homes themselves. I'm not sure I could go through that experience again. The job that summer, as it turned out, was extremely boring as we basically completed and filed reports all day long. And while it was one of the more boring jobs I've ever had, Kathy would take me to lunch, which was the highlight of each day. Sometimes Gina or other kids would join us, but typically, it was just me and Kathy. She would always ask me questions about the children's home and how I was doing.

The truth was that I was starting to rebel against my cottage parents and their rules. In bed each night, I continued to think about my situation: if I could get with a family, if I could live with them, it would help me adjust in the world. When I leave here, what's going to happen when I'm eighteen? I'm going to have to get a job or go to college. Who's going to pay for that? The state doesn't pay for any of that. I was obsessed about the future. I was only twelve, then thirteen, then fourteen but I thought about what my life would look like when I was nineteen, twenty, twenty-one. I could live with friends, yes, but I needed a foundation and that foundation had to be a family. I was just a cog in the wheel of life, and I would be out of NNCH at the age of eighteen and, apart from the work program, the home wasn't setting me up for life. I needed a family to nurture me and help me fulfill my potential. Not being seen as an individual was really starting to bother me. I was still focused on becoming a politician and needed to get to college. How was I going to get there?

Yes, my friends' parents liked me, and sometimes they even told me, "Hey, maybe we could see if you could come live with us?" But it never came to anything.

People were busy. They had lives and while I was welcome for a pool party on a Saturday afternoon, were they really going to contact Social Services on a Monday morning to adopt me? It didn't seem so. People are kind, they invite you to places, but that's only 10 percent of your life. The other 90 percent is still spent in a cinder block building with wood-paneled walls. No matter how great it is outside, I still had to come back to NNCH. I was still in jail. People loved me; I was nice and authentic, but I was sad too. I was also frustrated.

It might seem trivial, and maybe it was symbolic, but one of the things that annoyed me at the home was that we had to go to bed at 9:00 p.m., which was exactly when the good TV shows came on. Because it was lights out, I couldn't even read my *Sports Illustrated* magazine in bed. There was a TV mini-series called "V," which stood for visitors, and I wanted to watch it. It was about aliens who had visited earth and were eating humans. This sounded like quality entertainment to me! But to Lee, I'm sure it sounded completely ridiculous. Still, everyone at school was talking about the show and I didn't want to be left out.

One particular night, as a group of us sat watching TV, I could see that 9:00 p.m. was fast approaching. The television was against one wall, and we were all sitting facing it with the dining room behind us. This meant that we did not see Lee as he came up behind us. He walked over to the television and snapped it off, then wheeled around to face us, stating, "Gentlemen, good night!"

"Great, thanks for letting us watch the show!" I muttered and then proceeded to walk to my room.

This was the first time I had ever talked back to Lee, but I did it because I wanted some control over my life. This was quite different from Lee's plans for me. Having heard my sarcasm, he stepped in front of me, looking furious.

"What did you just say, young man?" he asked.

"I said 'great'," I said, my voice level as I made my way to bed. "We wanted to watch that show."

We went to bed that night as told but the subject of who controlled my life remained undefined. A couple of weeks later my very favorite show, *Moonlighting*, was airing a special two-hour episode built around Shakespeare's play *The Taming of the Shrew*. Together with the other boys in the cottage, we asked Lee if we could stay up late to watch it. But even though we were studying *Romeo and Juliet* at school, Lee saw no reason to bend his unbendable rules. I loved Shakespeare and since I also loved *Moonlighting*, this was the perfect mix for me. Once again, it was approaching 9:00 p.m. when Lee barged into the family room, walked straight over to the television, and turned it off with his usual phrase, "Goodnight, gentlemen."

There were six of us there and we sat for a moment, stunned. "Goodnight, gentlemen," he repeated.

We looked at each other. I couldn't believe it had happened again. "That's messed up," I said loudly, my hands folded across my chest.

Lee marched over to me and leaned into my face with his hands on his hips. "I am the law!" he shouted. "And you will do what you are told!"

"OKAY, LEE," I yelled and stormed to my room leaving him speechless and enraged that I had not used the term "Dad" or "Dad Wilhelm" as instructed.

"Go on. You heard me," he told the other boys, who hurried after me.

It was a big deal that I had called him Lee. I was asserting my independence. I was not going to back down. Later that night, Lee informed me that I was now on restriction and, as a result, could not be signed out to visit friends off campus and was forbidden from watching TV for a month.

The next day, I was still pissed, and I walked to work and explained to Kathy what had transpired. She listened attentively, having heard me complain about Lee on many occasions. "You need to start making decisions for yourself," she stated. I knew she was right.

"But how can I do that?" I asked. There was a pause.

"Steve," Kathy said. "Would you like to come live with Gina and me?"

I felt as if time was standing still. Shock, surprise, then a wave of joy passed through me. I looked down at my food, then slowly up at Kathy.

"Are you serious?" I asked her.

"Yes," she said. "Would you?"

I didn't hesitate. "Yes," I said.

A feeling of disbelief hit me. This was a nice gesture, but Kathy couldn't be serious, could she? My mind was reeling but the realities of how this might work out started to sink in. I knew that getting the home to approve her request was going to be a challenge since Kathy was a widow and had her own daughter to consider. A home that could offer me two parents was the ideal scenario in the eyes of the state. I stumbled back to my desk, thinking about how many children over the years had never gotten the chance to leave the home. That afternoon, I couldn't concentrate on my reports. Was I about to have a home? A family?

Back at the home, I went directly to my room, which I now had to myself as I was the longest residing child in the house. I lay down on my bed and reviewed all that had happened that day. I did not tell anyone in the cottage what Kathy had offered me. I was accustomed to failure and false hopes. Inside, I was beyond excited and delighted at the prospect of finally becoming part of a family. Kathy's offer to bring me into her family was one of the greatest moments of my young life, but I could not bring myself to show any emotion. I had been let down too many times. I lay on my bed, crossed my arms, looked up to the ceiling, and closed my eyes.

Dear God,

I cannot believe Kathy asked me to live with her and Gina. I know Brenda is not coming back for me. Please God, grant me this wish of a new family. I will behave and worship you.

In Jesus's name, amen.

* * *

The next day, Kathy asked me, "Aren't you at all excited about moving in with us?"

"I'm very excited," I said.

I was, of course, but I was so adept at concealing my true feelings that she couldn't tell. A few days later, I bumped into Gina. "Mom's really excited," she told me. "She's going to spoil you. Steve, this is going to be awesome. You're going to be my brother."

I heard Gina's words, but it was tough to believe them. I was fourteen years old and had experienced more pain, disappointment, and despair than most people experience in their entire lifetime. At that point in my life, another major disappointment could have sent me down a terrible path of self-destruction from which I may never have returned. I knew that. I knew I was not in the right place in the home. I had no doubt that after my recent battle with Lee, I may very well have headed back to juvenile hall and onto much worse. Some of it was the natural teenage striving for independence, but Lee was rigid, and I had begun to hate him and his controlling and condescending demeanor.

A few days later, the social worker Tom Hughes called me into his office at the home and asked me if I wanted to live with the Lopez family. I said that I did, but I still didn't feel confident it was going to happen. I would just accept whatever decision the state made. Because Kathy worked for the health facilities department, she knew exactly what she had to do to ensure that the state would approve her request to become my foster mother. Before the state came to inspect her home, she bought the requisite fire ladder and installed all the necessary safety features.

Still, the days waiting for a response from the state turned into weeks and then into months. I was still waiting to learn what my future would be.

CHAPTER TWENTY-FIVE

WASHINGTON, DC
JULY 1986

I heard static and then the voice of the bus driver came over the loudspeaker.

"Folks, I know some of you are from Los Angeles, but you have never seen traffic like The District."

"The District" was Washington, DC, and, according to our driver, Raymond, we should call it *The District* or people would think we were tourists. We were tourists, of course, but Raymond, a forty-year-old Black gentleman who had been our driver for our ten-day trip from Maryland to Virginia and then onto Washington, DC, didn't want us to appear that way.

The trip was organized by the Lutheran church in Carson that I occasionally attended. Starting in the fall of 1985, the church went on a fundraising spree to raise money for the trip, planned for the following summer, selling wrapping paper for the holidays or cookies for Valentine's Day. They hosted a spaghetti supper, car washes, raffles, and even a theater dinner with skits performed by the "Sun Shine Players."

On July 31, 1986, a group of eighteen young people, accompanied by Pastor Krumm, headed for Washington, DC, to be part of the fifteen thousand students attending the Lutheran Church-Missouri Synod (LC-MS) National Youth Gathering. Held every three years since 1980, the event provided numerous memorable and faith-lifting experiences with a focus on justice, freedom, and mercy. There was to be a gathering of thousands of students at the Washington Monument, who would then proceed on a Walk for Justice to the Lincoln Memorial, where a service was to be held around the reflecting pool.

I had made a friend at the church, Teri Case, whom I had a crush on, but our friendship ran deeper than that. We knew, without saying much to each other, that we were going through some of the same challenges in life. Unfortunately, she could not make the Washington, DC, trip. She had her own family stuff going on. We would remain friends and she would have a lasting impact on me.

Meanwhile, I was excited to be going on an airplane for the first time. I was also really interested in politics by this time, reading *The Christian Science Monitor*, *The New York Times*, and any political editorials I could get my hands on. Carson was a very political town, which influenced me a lot, and the chance to see the nation's capital, the seat of the federal government, was thrilling.

On the trip, we managed to pack in an impressive amount of sightseeing. We went to Williamsburg, the Smithsonian, the Washington Memorial, the Lincoln Memorial, the Tomb of the Unknown Soldier, the headquarters of *USA Today*, and other sites. We even attended a live video stream with then president Ronald Reagan, where he spoke about being a good citizen and a contributor to society, as well as being led by faith.

Given my extensive experience staying in run-down motels, the Howard Johnson and Marriott hotels were amazing to me, and I relished having my own room and a huge space. The room had a lovely carpet, and I even had my own key. Privacy! I could not believe my eyes when I spotted a telephone in the bathroom and at one point, a man knocked on the door and said, "Mr. Thompson, I've brought you some fresh towels." *Holy Toledo!* It was liberating just to be me, and to go down to dinner and eat alone if I wished.

I began to envision what my life could be if I was independent. I also realized that it would not be a huge leap for me to fit in with it all. I met kids from all over the country, including a cute girl from North Dakota who told me, "We have a small farm of 1,000 acres." I was like, that's not small! But it was eye-opening to chat freely and to just be me, and not be "Steve-From-The-Home." Many of these students had never been out of their home states either, but they were planning on attending colleges across the country and were enthusiastic about planning the next steps in their lives. It was inspiring, but still intimidating because I felt that everyone in DC looked at me like one of the members of the Cosby family. The truth is I did look a bit like "Theo Huxtable" from the TV show and occasionally, people would see me and shout, "Hey, Theo!"

On the last day of our trip, I was eager to see the Vietnam Veterans Memorial. As we approached it, our driver, Raymond, told us: "Folks, it has been a pleasure to be your guide this past week. You kids are great, and we are blessed to have you come and visit us here in The District." We all looked at each other and smiled, touched by his Southern hospitality and amused by his Louisiana drawl. But then his voice took on a serious tone. "This is the Vietnam Memorial," he said. "The Memorial is only four and a half years old. The names of 58,102 servicemen and women are etched on that wall over that hill.

It is said to be a beautiful dedication to the soldiers lost in that war."
He shook his head and said, "Please, please, do not ask me to go up
that walk with you. I have never visited that wall because I served in
Vietnam, and I lost a lot of friends over in 'Nam and their names are
on that wall. I just can't bear to see the names of my friends that did
not come home."

The bus had been brimming from excitement and laughter only
a couple minutes before, but now it fell silent as Raymond swung it
into the parking lot. When it had come to a standstill and he had
switched the engine off, he looked at us solemnly and said, "I hope
you can pay your respects for me."

We silently filed off the bus and into the sweltering air. After
Raymond's comments, I wasn't sure what I was going to see. We
moved up the slight hill and the black granite of the wall came into
view. I don't know what I was expecting but as we moved closer, I
could see women, men, and children lingering, staring intently at the
wall. I'd been to numerous memorials that week, but this one was
unlike any of the others. The dark wall was cold and glossy. Its black
granite towered over me. It seemed to be holding something back.
I descended the slightly inclined walkway, touching the countless
names. I could not believe how many there were. Some of the folks
standing at the wall looked old.

They wept as they ran their fingers tenderly across the names of
their loved ones. The blazing sun cast a strong glare and I could see
my face reflected in the wall. There was silence.

As I got back on the bus, Raymond was there.

"How was it?" he asked.

"Big," I said. "And powerful."

Raymond looked me square in the eyes. "Thank you, young man,
for taking the time to visit such an important memorial," he said.

"Thank you for taking us to see such an important monument," I said, and I shook his hand as he tipped his hat at me.

The trip to Washington changed my life in many ways. I enjoyed being together with all the other church kids. It was fun, but it felt significant to be part of a larger gathering. Not only were my horizons expanding—the states of the union seemed smaller and more accessible to me—but the Vietnam Veterans Memorial affected me a great deal. I started asking myself what direction I wanted my life to take. All those names on that marble wall—a lot of them, sadly—didn't have choices anymore. But I did, and I wanted to make the most of it. Raymond affected me too. On that trip, we learned he had served in the Vietnam War, and therefore declined to visit the memorial as it hurt him deeply on many levels. I didn't want to live my life with a shadow hanging over me like that. I didn't want to live my life thinking about Brenda.

* * *

When I got back to Carson, I was on a high from the trip and what I believed it meant for my future, but going back to the home, I felt my world become very small again. Lee was constantly nagging me, telling me his usual shit, and I was done with it. *When do I get out of here?*

A few weeks later, I started my sophomore year at Carson High and shortly after that, Kathy told me the magic words: "Steve, we're good to go. We're approved." I was stunned.

"Okay," I said, "I'm so happy. Thank you."

Kathy gave me a hug, but I was in shock. A million thoughts rushed through my mind. I went back to my cottage to lay on my bed.

This was it, the game changer. Did I know how to act? No. I guess I acted as I felt. Totally stunned.

Everything I wanted was coming to fruition. *How can I make this work? How will it be to live with just two people—both women?* It felt strange to be living at the home with the other children knowing that I would soon be leaving. I worked hard to maintain my composure, especially when I wanted to run about screaming, "I'm outta here, bitches, good luck!" I became quietly euphoric, but also prepared for it all to go wrong.

A couple of days later, one of my cottage brothers came over and told me that Lee wanted to see me in the office. I left my room and slowly walked to see him. I assumed that the move to Kathy's house was off and braced myself for the bad news.

When I got to the office, Lee and Barbara were both in there. Barbara sat down, and Lee stood with his hands on his hips, just as he did when he was going to lay down the law. I prepared myself for the bad news. *I'm a month away from my fifteenth birthday*, I told myself, *and I know that I am going to live at the home until I am eighteen.*

Barbara spoke first. "Stephen," she said, and paused. *This cannot be good.*

"It sounds like the Lopezes have been approved for you to live with them." I held my breath.

"Stephen," she said. "You never belonged here. You are a great kid. I really mean it. I've watched you grow over the years, and you have become quite a young man."

I was shocked. She continued, "You have so much potential, and I hope you take advantage of this opportunity. We thought you would probably live here until you were eighteen."

Lee spoke then. "You are getting an opportunity to start a new life for yourself, young man," he said. "Over the last couple of weeks your attitude has been anything but stellar. I suggest you leave that attitude here and not carry it with you to the Lopez home. You're very lucky that she was approved. I almost stopped it based on your recent attitude."

I held my breath again.

"However," he continued, "You don't belong here, and you never have. I am very proud of you for making a connection with this family and getting this truly unique opportunity. Still, don't screw it up, or you will be right back in that back bedroom waiting until you graduate."

*   *   *

On my last day at the home, I packed up the few things I had collected over the years. I had an extremely old radio that looked like it was made in the 1950s, some photographs dating from the time I moved into the home, and a few clothes. I picked up the cassette I had recorded at Great America. I had none of the typical things that celebrate a child's development and achievements. No cherished toys, videos, Little League trophies, blankets, or first shoes. I put what I had into a bag and a couple of boxes. I then walked around the grounds of the home and said goodbye to the people I called my extended family. I went to Cottage Six and said bye to my remaining friends there, then to the girls' cottages to tell them I was off. Then, as the sun was setting, Kathy arrived in her red Subaru sedan. I was sitting waiting in the living room and saw her arrive and pull into the parking lot.

"Okay," I said to Lee and Barbara, "Kathy's here."

She came inside and introduced herself to Lee and Barbara.

"I'll take your box, Steve," she said, and went back out to the car.

I turned and walked toward Barbara and gave her a long hug. Then, as if to let him know that I was a man now, I shook Dad Wilhelm's hand. I had been the longest resident of Cottage One. I got into the car and did not look back. Unlike the countless times I had moved previously in my life, this time I knew it was for real. I was moving in a positive direction for the first time in my life and I could feel it deep in my bones. Excitement pulsed through my veins as we drove across town to Kathy's home that had become so familiar to me over the past few years. I looked at Kathy and smiled. She smiled back.

When we got to the house that I knew so well, I climbed out of the car, smiled, and exhaled a breath that I felt I had been holding in all my life. I surveyed my new surroundings as Kathy quietly observed me. It was the first time Kathy saw how truly excited I was to begin my new life with her. I walked up the front stairs and through the front door, a threshold that I had crossed countless times in the past. But this was no longer just Gina's home; it was mine too.

"Put your things in the back bedroom," Kathy told me. I was to have Vince's room, Gina's older brother by five years who was off at college. It was large with a massive waterbed dominating the center of the room along with a large closet. "Just put your things anywhere you'd like. We'll go to the store later in the week so that you can pick out some furniture for your new room," Kathy said.

"Why? There's plenty of furniture in here already," I replied.

Finally having a room of my own in an actual home was more than enough for me. But Kathy insisted on getting some new furniture and looking back, I know that she wanted me to feel I had some control over my new life.

That night, I lay on my bed in my new room and stared at the ceiling. I had stared at a lot of bedroom ceilings in my life but this one felt good, and it felt permanent. I thought about my luck. Just the day before, I was living in a group home. Now I had been granted the very thing that I had spent so many nights praying for, a family of my own. I felt like I had hit the lottery. Relief, happiness, and guilt washed over me all at the same time. Relief to be out of the home, happiness at having found Kathy and Gina, and guilt for what this meant for Dana, who was still out there on his own. I called him to let him know where I was.

RENO
THE BIGGEST LITTLE CITY IN THE WORLD

Hotel
Goodbyes

CHAPTER TWENTY-SIX

When I woke up, not for the first time in my life, I couldn't remember where I was. But then I moved, felt the waterbed, remembered, and smiled. I had only moved a few miles, but I was in a different world. I stepped onto the carpet, put my sweatpants on, and walked down the hall to the bathroom.

"Steve, do you want something to eat?" Kathy called out. It was a Saturday morning, and the weekend was stretching ahead of me.

"Yes, please," I called back.

It dawned on me that Kathy had never had a foster child and I wasn't the typical one. Most foster kids have some kind of relationship with their biological families. I did not. My closest sibling was Dana and he lived miles away. I had no parents or other relatives. This meant that Kathy and Gina and her brother, Vince, now constituted my family.

It is not easy to join a new family. It is not like a plant on which you just pour water, and it grows. It is a very special challenge. I was aware that Kathy had made a momentous decision that would enable me to grow up in her household. Obviously, she wasn't doing it for the money; four hundred dollars a month is a drop in the bucket when it comes to providing financially for a growing adolescent boy. I believe Kathy simply wanted to give me an extraordinary opportunity. Did she want me? After all, she had children of her own. It never occurred to me that I was wanted, that Kathy wanted me to be her son. For now, I was welcome to live with her, and since that brief moment living with Aunt Ouida and Uncle Jerry, this was the first time that I wasn't living somewhere where I was merely required to stay.

That first week, Kathy gave me a set of rules. They were very simple. I had no curfew, no set bedtime, and no rules regarding my homework. I did have to do my own laundry and some chores around the house. Other than that, I was not going to be told what to do on a daily basis. Initially, this freedom, implicitly intertwined with responsibility, felt overwhelming. They were in complete contradiction to the copious restrictions of life under Lee Wilhelm. At the home, I was told when to get up, how long to shower, what to eat, what time to go to school, how long to study, and when to go to bed. I was given a specific day when I could do my laundry and was assigned to clean the kitchen and bathrooms on certain nights. I could only use the phone thirty times per week. There was no flexibility. If my homework took longer to complete than the assigned hour, I had no choice but to stop studying and go to bed. At the home, no one cared about the grades I earned in school, only that I completed my work in the allotted amount of time. In contrast, at Kathy's household, I was given freedom to organize and conduct my life. I quickly noticed that she never checked on my homework. So, one day I asked her, "Aren't you going to check and make sure my homework is done?"

Kathy and Gina laughed.

"Steve, it's up to you," Kathy said. "You are welcome to fail, if you want. I'm not going to make you do your homework. That's your responsibility."

This was the opportunity I wanted—not to be governed but to determine my own path. At first, I imagined that I would not have to study anymore or care about my grades. However, I quickly realized that I wanted to get good grades for myself, not for anyone else. It was a significant revelation. After dinner, I would watch TV with Gina for as long as I liked. I still didn't have all the control I wanted, however, since Gina watched basically nothing but musicals—*Chorus Line* on VHS for example. If I had too much of TV musicals, I'd move to my bedroom to read my science or English homework. But it was hard to get up and leave the TV room. Gina was always dancing around, and we were having fun chilling together. Still, I knew I had to study. In the end, I think I was a good role model to Gina who was more interested in dancing, cheerleading, modeling, and acting, rather than studying.

Some years later, Kathy told me that when I'd moved in, she was shocked by how much I asked her what I should do. She was perplexed that I required so much guidance related to the most mundane aspects of my life and shocked at how the strict rules in the NNCH home had resulted in my having severely limited skills for handling my daily living.

Soon after I settled in, Kathy gave me one more instruction. She sat me down on the living room couch and said, "Do not get arrested, Steve, because I am not going to bail you out." I nodded. It was crystal clear that Kathy was going to treat me like an adult.

I had no intention of getting arrested. I had admired Uncle Jerry's side hustle of selling weed to give his family a better lifestyle and knew that I wanted to have and provide the stability that he had created. But I also knew what a life of crime looked like, thanks to Brenda and Gus. As a young Black man, going to prison was always a fear, so I didn't need any more incentives to avoid a life of crime. I'd seen it up close when I was in juvey. I was very firm on which path I wanted to walk. I'd been a student of human behavior. I knew what I wanted from life.

I still loved to read and devoured a book that Kathy gave me called *Native Son* by Richard Wright. The book, set in the South Side of Chicago in the 1930s, centers on a Black character, Bigger Thomas, who is uneducated and poor and who makes a terrible mistake. The book is very powerful and, while reading it, I began to ponder the many similarities between Bigger and myself. Kathy had given me the book without any insight or proclamations. Maybe she was telling me something. Maybe she wanted to motivate me to strive harder and farther.

Kathy, whose maiden name was Ramirez, was born in Los Angeles in 1942, the oldest of five girls. Her father was a Mexican immigrant, a painter by talent and a handyman by trade, who would take odd jobs all over the city. He enjoyed painting and was very interested in political causes of special importance to Mexican Americans. Like all her sisters, Kathy really loved her father. However, her mother was a different story. Originally from Georgia and of German and Polish heritage, Kathy's mother was very strict and tough on all her daughters and was particularly cruel to Kathy. The Ramirez family was very poor and lived in a very small home that Kathy's father had built by himself. Kathy and her four sisters slept in a room that she described as a closet with three racks of beds. Kathy oversaw her younger sisters and would spend many hours and days watching over them and caring for them. Kathy had a very difficult relationship with her mother, who may have resented the strength and determination in Kathy and her unwillingness to settle.

Their relationship was fractured by verbal and physical abuse. The similarities between Kathy and me were extremely evident even though we shared no DNA. Kathy saw something that many others did not see in me, and she also saw something much more. She may have recognized herself in me. The hiding of emotions, the deep distance from others, even friends. However, my sheer determination and belief in my own convictions must have also struck a familiar chord in her. Kathy knew that by giving me freedom to conduct my life the way I wanted, it would open me up to certain risks, the risk of failure. However, she also knew that if she was too strict, I would take too few risks, which would limit my exposure to the realities of life and hinder my ability to reach my full potential. Instead, by giving me a protective framework with few limitations, Kathy was laying the groundwork that would enable me to become prepared for managing my own life without a safety net.

I began to feel very comfortable at Kathy's home. It was different living with two women rather than with a load of boys—the house smelled nice for a start. But it wasn't too long before it really started to feel like my actual home, and it was a good feeling. It didn't take long to start enjoying my new life, a lot. Things were looking up for me. Years later, I would spend much of my professional life recruiting talent to top companies. At the time, although I didn't realize it, I had in a sense recruited myself a family.

RENO
THE BIGGEST LITTLE CITY IN THE WORLD

Hotel Goodbyes

CHAPTER TWENTY-SEVEN

"My name is Stephen Thompson, and I am running for class president because I want to bring the passion back to our class!"

There was an excited roar. I continued, "I am running not to bring in Coke machines or gum, but because I want us to bring the spirit back to this school. In three years, I want us to have left our footprint. I look across this room and I see passion and determination. We are the class of 1989, and we will not be forgotten!"

Shortly after I moved into Kathy's house, Gina and her girlfriends began managing my campaign for class president of my tenth-grade class in high school. I had mentioned to Kathy that I might be interested in running as I had always wanted to be an elected official. The next thing I knew, Gina and her friends added my name to the list of candidates, made posters and flyers, and hung them all around the school.

As I sat waiting to make my speech to an enormous hall full of students, I was incredibly nervous, and it seemed an eternity before my opponent stepped up to the podium and began to address our classmates first. As I listened, I realized that she lacked passion and conviction. She spoke about the typical junior high stuff like promising to get the administration to install Coke machines in the cafeteria or how much she cared about the students. I studied the crowd. I knew from watching preachers capture the imagination of their congregation, or from football coaches giving motivational speeches, that I had to grab the mic and be as passionate as possible. I knew the first sentence had to grab attention and that when it came to the second sentence, I had to slow down and speak as if I was just chatting to a friend. Effective public speakers, I believed, needed to come off as knowledgeable and comfortable and display an infectious energy.

The crowd cheered as I sat down after my speech. What I'd said was true—our class was famous for displaying tremendous spirit for our athletes as well as for having exceptional students, and I wanted to display that same passion in my speech, unlike my opponent. My vice president, John Kinsey, stood up next.

"Exactly what he said!" said John, grinning at me. The crowd erupted in laughter.

I got up from my chair and felt good about my speech. It was heartfelt and what I believed. Several of my friends gave me a pat on the back and said I'd done a great job. My opponent did not look at me and walked away. I felt bad at that point. I knew she really wanted to be class president.

The voting happened the next day and the day after that, the results were announced. I'd won in a landslide. "I knew you would win," Kathy told me, and Gina was so proud. Winning that tenth-grade election would set the bar for my next two years at Carson High School.

At home, I was getting used to my relationship with Gina and Kathy and learning the unwritten rules such as where to put my shoes or when to do the laundry. I'm sure they were getting used to me too. I began to perceive that I had a different relationship with Kathy than Gina did. In hindsight, that should have been obvious, but at first it made me uncomfortable. Of course, Kathy did treat me differently from the way she treated Gina, but only because I was a young boy, who she needed to mold into a man in a relatively short period of time. Gina, on the other hand, was her only daughter, whom she had raised her entire life. To a new foster child, it is very difficult to comprehend and accept this intimate connection as it is usually something they have not experienced themselves. I was eager for Kathy's approval, and I started to get mildly jealous of Gina despite the fact that I knew better, having seen my friends go through similar conflicting emotions with their adoptive families.

There was one minor incident when Gina and I were wrestling in the living room. I was doing what I was accustomed to doing with my guy friends at the home. Without thinking, I threw her against the couch. I really did not intend on tossing her as hard as I did; however, she flew up in the air and crashed into the back of the couch and it broke with a thunderous clunk.

"Oh shit! Are you all right?" I asked.

"Mom is going to kill us!" she said.

We decided it would be best to confess what happened rather than trying to cover it up. Later that week, Kathy told me that she needed to have a discussion with me regarding the couch-breaking incident. She was very direct and stern and made it very clear that she would not tolerate that kind of behavior.

"Do you like living here?" she asked bluntly, looking straight at me. "Do you want to go back to the home?"

This was one of the first and only times that Kathy criticized or disciplined me, and I was scared. I knew that this kind of behavior was not going to be tolerated. She was serious about sending me back if I ever did something like that again. I told her I was very happy living there and that it would never happen again.

"I'm sorry," I said.

"I know," she responded.

I looked at her. There was a question I desperately needed the answer to.

"Do you think my mother, Brenda, was a good person?" I asked.

I'm sure most fifteen-year-olds ask searching questions about who they are or who they want to be. But my questions were different. A large part of me was still questioning my decision to call for help in that Reno motel room, and I still felt guilty for betraying Brenda and for being the one responsible for dispersing my siblings across California and Nevada. Kathy also had a mother that she did not want to replicate. I knew she could understand my pain and answer this question. She didn't hesitate.

"Yes," she said. "She had you and you are a smart and kind person. Steve, you will not be like her."

I think we both knew that she was saying this to reassure me, a bewildered young man trying to find a way to believe in himself, but her simple answer caused me to let go of my need to gain approval from Brenda. While she would never know it, Brenda transplanted all her future responsibilities for me onto Kathy that day. There was no exchange of words or signing of papers. I simply silently transitioned from being Brenda's native son to being Kathy's chosen son. I began calling her "Mom." It was partly because that's what Gina called her, so it became natural for me to refer to Kathy in the same way. But also because it felt right.

CHAPTER TWENTY-EIGHT

SUMMER 1988
LAKE TAHOE

I n the summer between my junior and senior year in high school, I went on a beach trip to Zephyr Cove, Lake Tahoe, with my friend Kip Perry. The youngest of the Perry clan, Kip was a Native Nevadan, which was somewhat unusual in a state with so many transplants from somewhere else. The Perry family had a long history as ranchers in rural Yerington, Nevada, and Kip's father and uncles became high-profile attorneys in the Silver State. Vic Perry, Kip's dad, was a very strong-willed and determined person, someone who was extremely focused but also loved to take risks.

I first met Kip years ago when John Kinsey and I were teaching a breakdancing class at the Capital Courts membership club. Kip was a tiny guy, but he had some decent moves and could break well. John and I gave him some tips and Kip went to work practicing on the hardwood floor in the basketball gym. I remember Kip wore a Carson City High T-shirt, which was notable to me because I had never owned one and I knew they were pretty expensive, at least for my limited funds. Kip was a cute, energetic, and nice kid, just a pleasure to be around. Because he was so small, I had no idea that he was only a grade behind me in school.

A couple of months after first meeting him at the club, we were reintroduced by our mutual friend Melissa Smith. Kip was also friends with John Wurster, Curt Worlund, and Paul Kenne. All of us would stay friends.

Kip and I became better friends after I moved in with the Lopez family. Eventually, I ended up meeting Kip's entire family as I became a frequent guest at Kip's house. His family has been extremely kind to me over the years, and I loved eating his mother's Swedish pancakes with bacon on the side whenever I spent the night. I learned a lot from Kip and his family as I did from most of my friends and their families. These families joked with each other, played games, went on vacations, and had arguments—all in front of me. All families celebrate as well as fight and that is normal. What I learned from my experiences is that families stay together. This is not a shocking revelation to those with families. However, when your life does not have this fundamental pillar, you notice it when it's missing.

In high school, Kip and I went to the beach at Lake Tahoe, attended countless parties, and played football together. Kip was a great wrestler and wanted to play football. He tried out his junior year and did well. During our trip to Zephyr Cove, Kip and I sat on the beach in our lawn chairs and just looked out at the crystal clear waters that are the hallmark of any Tahoe experience. That day it was hot as usual, and the scent of pine trees filled the air. The sound of the water quietly lapping along the shoreline had a soothing effect as I dug my toes deep into the white sand. The sand at Zephyr Cove, although hot, is soft and smooth as it does not contain any rocks unlike most harbors or Nevada beaches. I picked up a cold beer and took a long sip. It was a cool relief on this hot summer day. Kip told me that he would love to work on a beach. I nodded in agreement thinking to myself, *Yeah, why not?*, as it was so peaceful and scenic along the shore. On a whim, I suggested, "Let's buy a bar someday."

"Yeah … in San Diego," Kip concurred. Then he added, "Have you ever been to San Diego?"

"Nope," I replied, taking another swig of my beer. Kip went on to explain that although Tahoe is a great town with scenic views that match the lake, it wouldn't be a great place for a bar, in his opinion.

"Maybe you and I should go to college in San Diego," he said.

I sat silent for a while, just contemplating what Kip had suggested. For the next couple of minutes, we just sat there in silence, enjoying the beauty around us. My mind was churning as I mulled over the possibilities for my future. I had been considering going to Oregon or Northern California for college, but the past winter had been a cold one for Nevada and was making me reconsider whether I wanted to be around the cold any longer. We clinked our beers together and agreed this might have been the best day at the beach yet.

The next month was great as Kip's parents were out of the country and we played like rock stars at his house in Carson City. Kip's home was a large redwood home with twenty-foot windows with a huge family room with a pool table and video games. He also had a TV room with all the best music equipment along with a beautiful deck with a hot tub on it. His home was basically our bar that month with all our friends coming over to hang out each night. That month of fun at Kip's house represented the end of our summer vacation, but it certainly was not the end of our journey together.

* * *

As football practice got started that August before my senior year, *USA Today* visited our campus to interview students for a piece about life at a regular American high school. I was very interested in taking part because during my previous trip to Washington, DC, with my Lutheran Church, I had the opportunity to visit the *USA Today* offices and was enthralled watching the process of how a newspaper got made.

Now the newspaper was coming to our Carson City High School and columnists spent the week interviewing various students about their experiences. No one had interviewed me yet, but on Friday night, my football coach called my house and told me to be at the football field the next morning by 8:00 a.m. and to bring my jersey so that *USA Today* could take some pictures.

I agreed and got up early the next morning to prepare to go over to the field. Teresa Diloreto, who was a good friend of Gina's, pulled up in front of our house in her BMW. A cheerleader, gymnast, track star, and student government leader, Teresa was going to the University of Colorado-Boulder after high school. We arrived at the field where, to my surprise, there were only a handful of cars in the parking lot and just two other people there—OJ Sanchez and Teresa. OJ was one of my teammates and now as we headed into our senior year, he was also the student body president for the entire school. Teresa and OJ already knew where they were going to college, with OJ heading off to the US Air Force Academy and Teresa to Boulder. But I was still unsure where I would end up because for me the college process was just beginning. After some small talk and a few jokes, Kent, the *USA Today* photographer, got up on a ladder and shouted, "Crowd together!" Teresa, OJ, and I inched closer together. With the sun blaring into our eyes, we put on big smiles for the camera. "Good. One more …" Kent said before exclaiming, "Nice. We got it!" It was hot and we were ready to be done with photos.

The next morning, I woke up to hear the telephone ringing. I looked up to see Gina grab the telephone receiver and shout, "Hello?" It was quiet for a moment while she listened to the person on the other end of the line. I was half asleep as I was sore and tired from our football game the previous night. After spending a few hours smashing into people as a linebacker your body just aches and all I wanted to do was lay down and drink Gatorade. I lay there on the couch covered in two blankets. I had been known to lay on the couch and sleep for days. Over the years, the couch had morphed into my bed since it was the most comfortable spot in the house. I then heard Gina say, "Hey, Anthony! Oh my God … good. How are you? Yes, hold on." She yells over to me, "Steve, it's AV on the phone."

AV was short for Anthony Vollet, a former classmate of ours who was now in college at UNLV. Anthony was a year older, and we had played track and football together at Carson High. AV was a great guy and he and I used to hang out with two other people from his class, Carlos Mendeguia and Spencer Mellum. Now, they were all off at college and I was the one holding down the fort. I grabbed the phone. "Yo, yo, what are you up to, Mr. Vollet?" I said into the phone.

"So, I am walking down the street in Las Vegas, and I walk by a newsstand and I look," begins AV. "Then I look again. And I see you on the cover of the *USA Today*!"

I laughed and said, "Yeah, after you left, the press wanted to come here and cover some real stars!" We both laughed.

Anthony told me that he was getting the bug to play football again, but he didn't think he could play at UNLV. He said that he was thinking of moving to San Diego to attend Mesa College. "Why Mesa?" I asked. He said it has a good football program and, since it was a junior college, students can complete all their basic requirements and then transfer to a California state school for their last two years.

Anthony then said something simple yet profound, as it would change the trajectory of my future in a radical way: "I am coming home in a couple of weeks. Maybe we should talk about you going there with me next year and we can play together? It would be just like the good ol' days." *Interesting*, I thought to myself. I had just taken the ACT exam the other day and boy was that a horrible experience. I was sure I failed miserably so maybe going to a junior college in California would be a good idea. I could play football and work on my grades. *I'm liking this plan more and more*, I thought to myself as I hung up the phone.

A couple of weeks later Anthony showed up in Carson, just as he promised, and he and I hung out. He told me that he had decided to move to San Diego ahead of time to establish his California residency so that he could be eligible for in-state tuition, meaning that instead of paying $2,200 per year, he would only have to pay just $1,100. After listening to him, it became clear to me that Mesa College could be a very viable option for me in terms of affordability. I decided it was an option I would consider as I pondered my future.

CHAPTER TWENTY-NINE

"Stephen," the guidance counselor explained, "your grades simply aren't strong enough for college to be an option for you."

I had adjusted to my new life as an "adopted" child in Kathy's home, and I was thriving. I had been a popular class president in my sophomore year and right before my senior year, I was voted by my teammates as defensive captain of my football team. It was a huge honor, and I was stunned. I had also appeared on the pages of a national newspaper. But not everyone, it seemed, was on my side. I looked at my guidance counselor.

"What do you mean?" I asked.

"What I mean is that you should consider a trade, not college," she said. "I'm sorry, but college just isn't in the cards for you. You'll never make it at that level."

My English teacher had asked the guidance counselor to speak with me. I planned to be a lawyer as I knew it was a well-trodden route to politics. But I was really struggling in English and was writing papers that were bad by any standard. I had the fundamentals and was verbally articulate, but I struggled to get my viewpoint across in writing.

In addition, I knew the counselor was still upset that it was her daughter whom I ran against and beat in the election for sophomore class president. I sat there in her stuffy office and stared at her, the person that was supposed to be encouraging me as I planned for my future. Even though I was in shock, there was no question in my mind that I was going to college, with or without her support. This would be the first of many statements by many people in my life including well-meaning friends' parents, teachers, students, and acquaintances who would often suggest that I should set lower expectations, that I should stay in my place, due to my perceived "underprivileged background."

"Why don't we think of something more fitting for someone from your background," she said. "What about plumbing?"

"A plumber?" I repeated.

"Yes," she said. "That's a profession that you could enter fairly quickly after some training."

It wasn't the worst suggestion. Plumbers are skilled and earn a good living. But it wasn't the profession she had suggested that had offended me; it was that she was trying to discourage my dream of attending college. How many other kids from NNCH did she similarly try to dissuade from their dream of a higher education?

And conversely, how many students who were not from NNCH did she try to push into something that they had no desire to do? I refused to accept her lowered expectations for me and decided I would follow my own path. Why would I listen to her? It wasn't as if I had always been surrounded by stellar adults dishing out sage advice. I grew up to question what most adults told me.

The guidance counselor didn't know me and hadn't been through what I had been through. She didn't know me like I knew me. Or like Kathy knew me. She didn't know that I wanted to go into politics. On the one hand, I discounted everything the counselor said to me that day. But, on the other hand, she also gave me a great gift. I am sure she was only trying to help me the best way she knew by setting the bar low so that I wouldn't fail and get discouraged. It was as if she had put a broom on the ground and dared me to jump over it.

I sat listening to the counselor as she offered other ideas for how my life might turn out. I drifted away, wondering if Senator Neal had been right: Is the system set up for kids like me to fail, a Black kid from a children's home? But I also wondered, what was the real risk of spending my time trying to obtain something that might not be a possibility? I asked myself this and could not think of a single thing. There was no risk in trying. Failure could be either the end result or just the beginning. *What happens afterward if you fail in your quest to go to college, Stephen?* Nothing.

According to my guidance counselor, I have nothing and can be nothing. So, what was the risk? There wasn't one. Could I turn failure into risk and possibly into success? Finally, I rose determinedly from my chair and looked at my guidance counselor with contempt and disgust.

"Thank you, Mrs. Counselor," I said.

And I walked out, leaving her low expectations behind me.

CHAPTER THIRTY

The summer before our senior year, Gina and I thought it would be good for Mom to go out and meet people. She was not very interested, but Gina and I, along with her closest friend, Diana, finally convinced her. On her first night out, she ended up meeting Ray, who happened to attend my church. It was the first and only night she ventured out as they hit it off like two peas in a pod and started to spend a lot of time together. In fact, they spent so much time together, usually at Ray's house, that Gina and I were basically living by ourselves. Typically, Mom would leave around 8:00 p.m. and return very early in the morning to make sure we were up and ready for school. She would also clean around the house and make sure we had enough groceries in the pantry. She was often away on weekends as well, and Gina and I quickly got used to our freedom. We spent our time listening to music from Prince or terrifying ourselves silly by watching movies like *Night of the Living Dead* or *Friday the 13th.*

Since Gina was a cheerleader and very popular, there would always be kids over at our house. We had a reputation for having a very cool pad in which to hang out. During the week, we would get home and various friends would already have let themselves in to sit on the couch and watch TV.

Given how many kids were routinely at our house, I started to think that Gina and I should formalize this arrangement and host parties to make a little money. We thought through all the logistics. We knew all the kids in the school and since I was a starting outside linebacker on the football team and was friends with all the players, we knew we wouldn't have to worry about any fights. Gina also happened to be very good friends with Nicole, whose father was a sergeant in the Carson City Sheriff's Department, so we could always call on him for backup if things got out of hand. Gina and I agreed on some basic party rules. We would only invite kids aged sixteen and older; we would provide two kegs of beer; and we would sell each partygoer a cup for five dollars. We managed to procure the kegs using a variety of different methods. The first option was to find an adult willing to buy one for us. They cost seventy-five to eighty-five dollars. If this did not work, we would simply go to the grocery store, walk into the cooler, grab one or two kegs, and simply walk out. Grocery store clerks weren't so vigilant in those days, but it was still just one of those dumb things that kids do!

One of the most important party rules was that kids were not allowed to park on our street. We wanted the street to be clear if the cops were called, so that they might not be able to identify which house was hosting the party. That was my idea. If the party was loud and the cops came, we would send Nicole out to talk to them, and she would inform them who her father was and usually the cops would leave us alone after telling us to quiet down. The parties would end at midnight, at which time I would kick out most of the guests. We would then tap the second keg and share it with about twelve to fifteen kids who were staying over. We would also order pizza, which was generally free since Domino's, who had a policy of free pizza if your delivery was late, never seemed to arrive on time. At the end of the night, Gina and I would split the profit, which would usually amount to around $150. We threw these parties every other month. It was a pretty good take for two kids and clearly there was an element of creativity and rule breaking necessary to turn a profit. What would Lee Wilhelm have said?

"Barbara! Write him up."

RENO

THE BIGGEST LITTLE CITY IN THE WORLD

Hotel Goodbyes

CHAPTER THIRTY-ONE

I had enjoyed three incredible years of family life with Gina and Kathy. But I knew that if I could not go back to Kathy's once I graduated from high school, then I would have to go to college with a long-term work plan in place. If I was going to live at college, and work while I was there, I would have to go somewhere not very expensive, such as the University of Nevada at Reno. However, I dreamed of exploring somewhere new and if I could stay with Mom each summer, then I would be able to save on a couple of month's rent and work in town to earn funds for the upcoming school year.

Further education, and how it's paid for in the United States, is complicated. Each state has its own way of arranging its finances and most of them fund public universities, along with vocational or junior colleges. Some of these junior colleges offer general studies so that students can then get into a four-year university. Most states fund their own state system to do this and provide much lower tuition to in-state residents. Obviously, some state schools are outstanding. There are also countless private universities that get federal grants from the national government, and students can receive grants, scholarships, or financial aid to help pay for tuition. If I had wanted to go to UCLA for example, that would have been out-of-state tuition, although being from a foster home meant that I was at least entitled to some additional funding.

I wanted to study political science in college, but I also wanted to play football. I wasn't getting recruited and did not expect to receive an athletic scholarship, but I thought back to my conversation with AV, Anthony Vollet, about Mesa College. He was loving his time there, both in the classroom and on the football field, and still encouraging me to consider it. The football program and the general education were good and, if you did well at a junior college in California, you could transfer to a University of California school, such as UCLA or Cal Berkeley, which would be a huge deal.

In the spring of my senior year, my mom, her boyfriend Ray, Gina, and I took a road trip to San Diego to explore college options. Gina and I stayed with AV, and he took us around to the various campuses including his own Mesa College, San Diego State University, University of California at San Diego, San Diego City College, Grossmont Junior College, and the University of San Diego (USD)—a smaller Catholic college nestled in the hills just northwest of downtown. We ended up spending a couple of hours at USD since John Eck, a Carson High alumnus, was studying there. It's consistently rated as one of the most beautiful campuses in the country and with 300 days of sunshine, it was irresistible. John Eck would eventually become one of my closest friends. He had three older brothers in college, and he would have to get a scholarship to attend college. USD had offered him the scholarship he needed. Unfortunately, USD or other four-year colleges were not in the cards for me, at least not yet, so with AV's urging and support, I decided to attend Mesa College.

* * *

Before any of this, in April 1989, in preparation for starting college that September, I needed to ask my mom a question. She came home one night, and I sat at the counter in the kitchen and watched her prepare dinner. We exchanged some small talk and then I took a deep breath and said, "Mom, after I go to college, would it be all right if I come back here to stay with you for the summer?"

Her back was toward me as she stood over the stove making my favorite tacos. She turned around, holding a wooden spatula in her hand, looked me dead in the eye, and said, "You're always welcome to come home." She then turned back to stirring the ground beef, seasoning it as it sizzled in the pan. "Steve," she asked, as she had on so many nights, "how many tacos do you want?"

A wave of relief washed over me. She had just uttered the words that I had longed to hear. My mother knew my fears and she had allayed them in an instant.

* * *

A few weeks later, the day had come: high school graduation. June 1989. I had waited patiently for Gina to get ready every morning for three years. She was always late. But this time, she was ready to go right on time. We looked at each other as we stood in the kitchen. It was a special day for us. We both knew that we wouldn't have many more of these moments together. Gina had done so much to get to where she was as a cheerleader, as an actress, and as a dancer, along with nominations for homecoming queen. She had grown into a beautiful young woman. I was very proud of her because she wanted to dance and would not accept anything less than that as part of her life plan.

There was a knock at the door. I opened it and Pat, Gina's date, and Lori, my date, came inside. Lori had been in Carson for a couple of years. She had rich blue eyes and wonderful dirty-blond hair that hung below her shoulders. She had a stunning figure, and I'd had a crush on her for years. It was never going to be reciprocated but at least she agreed to come to graduation as my date.

I opened the fridge and grabbed four cold Coors Lights. No Keystone Lights today—this was a special occasion—and this would be the first of many beers that day. As we arrived at Carson High School, it was sweltering. We took our seats on the field. The metal stands were crowded with people, friends, family, and even members of the community; there must have been ten thousand people there.

My football teammate and friend, Matt Smith, one of four valedictorians in the class, was delivering the roll call for diplomas, and he and I had come up with a special way for him to announce my name. When the speeches about our future were over, it was diploma time, although with diplomas handed out alphabetically and with a surname beginning with "T," I knew I was in for a long wait.

Matt read the names: "Brian Terrell," he called to clapping and cheering. Then, I saw Matt glance down at the name sheet and then look up at me. We both knew we could get in trouble, but we were done with high school. Our eyes met and Matt yelled, "Stephen. Jon. Earl. Air. Sweet T ... Thompson!" Jon is my middle name and "Earl" was my nickname given to me by my football friends. My legs were so big, 36 inches round, that I could not wear jeans and I could squat 650 pounds five times, so the name was given to me in honor of Earl Campbell, a running back who won the 1977 Heisman Trophy. "Air" was my nickname on the track team. It was somewhat unique in that I competed in so many different events including the shot put, the 100-meter dash, the 400-meter dash, the mile relay, and even the high jump, which was certainly not my strongest event. "Air" came about because I didn't like the idea of the high jump, so sometimes I would just sprint to the high jump pit and fail to jump. "Sweet T" was given to me as a term of endearment and certainly went well with Thompson.

My heart pounded and my face broke into a huge grin as I walked forward to the screaming cheers of my classmates and my mom and sister. I felt as if I was floating in the air as I took my diploma in my hand and marveled at what was usually a fairly ordinary accomplishment but for me, a former ward of the state and foster child, was an almost unfathomable achievement. It was a moment I had envisioned for years, and I felt triumphant. There had been many times when I didn't think I'd ever see the inside of a classroom again. And now, my next stop was college.

Hotel
Goodbyes

CHAPTER THIRTY-TWO

I went to San Diego two weeks after I graduated from high school to look for a job and get involved in the football summer league so that I could be ready to play in the fall at Mesa College. I moved into a two-bedroom apartment with John Eck.

My first semester at Mesa was tough. Everything was new and unfamiliar, even for me, someone who was used to moving around to new places. I had to learn where my classes were and which buses to take to get there. My classes, with fifty to one hundred students in them, weren't easy and the atmosphere was a big leap from high school. I was navigating all of this while trying to play football. I also worked nights on campus answering phones. It sucked because our apartment was miles from the Mesa campus. I didn't like it at all. I went from a life that I could manage to one that was tough to adapt to.

I was homesick and since Mesa College was a popular junior college in San Diego, it was also reasonably expensive, at least for me.

I was pretty poor, and while my friends weren't rich, they had parental support. Kathy was amazing, but she was still a single working mother trying to support her own daughter in college. There was only so much she could do for me, and I didn't want to be a burden. So, while my other friends went out for burgers and beer, I was working the phones, then boiling potatoes and wrapping them in foil for my lunch.

School, football, and work, all while hungry, was tough and I lost a ton of weight. But some of my friends had meal tickets, which their parents had credited with $2,000 at the start of the year, so they would share meals with me. Others gave me lifts when I needed them or they would recommend me for jobs they'd heard about. I found it hard to accept their help at times, but I was grateful to have a community of friends and support around me. I found studying tough and occasionally wanted to quit. My high school friend, Frank "The Tank" Grainer, was playing football at Mesa as well and he told me: "You can't quit something you've started." That made a big impression on me, and I persevered and made it through that first year, grateful for the encouragement.

I spoke to my mom every couple of weeks. It was expensive to call back then. It was never the case that she was going to help me financially. I always knew it was going to be me who had to pay, but I needed Kathy for mental support. Also, for those times when I was out of college—staying with her, having a home I could return to, was key.

It was fine; I borrowed money a couple of times. I was determined to study politics, go to law school, and become a US senator. I received some minor grants from the federal government and took out some student loans. But the funds were limited and the loans needed to be paid back when I was done with college. At the end of my freshman year, I moved back to Carson for the summer and worked for the Carson City School District, where I worked as a janitor. It was Mr. Courtright, the father of my high school friend, Chris Courtright, who got me the summer job. Chris was attending college at the US Naval Academy.

That summer, I spent a lot of time with Kip Perry, who had just graduated from Carson High. He was heading to San Diego for college as well, just as he and I had dreamed about at Zephyr Cove a year before.

While we both still agreed that San Diego was the right place to live and go to school, I decided to take a brief detour and attend the University of Nevada Las Vegas (UNLV) for a year. Gina and some other people I knew were going there, and I felt it would be the right spot for me for my sophomore year in college. Gina had spent her first year at Sierra Nevada University in Tahoe. But after she finished her first year, and after I had completed a year at Mesa, we decided to go to school together at UNLV. Gina was going to major in dance as Las Vegas would provide her with numerous opportunities to audition and perform. I decided to attend UNLV because out-of-state tuition in California was becoming just too expensive, even at a junior college, and because I was a Nevada state resident, the in-state tuition at UNLV was far more affordable.

My sophomore year at UNLV proved to be a great year for me as my good friends from high school, Carlos, Spencer, and Dan, were also attending UNLV and I was excited to watch the Running Rebels play basketball all season long. In 1990 when basketball season began, the Rebels were ranked number one in preseason and predicted to win the NCAA tournament. And, why not since they had beaten Duke the year before by thirty points in the NCAA finals. The Rebels that year were stacked with great players including Anderson Hunt, Stacy Augmon, George Achles, Greg Anthony, Everic Gray, Elmore Spence, and, of course, Larry Johnson.

All the players on the team were treated like superstars in Vegas. I did not have much interaction with the team, but I did have a class with Larry Johnson, who showed up about five to ten minutes late just about every day. One day, I was also running late to class, hustling from the other side of campus trying to make it on time. I was running up the stairs when I ran into Larry. Of course, at 6'6" with enormous shoulders, Larry was larger than life. He was moving slowly up the stairs as I rounded the corner and almost ran right smack into him. I slowed down a bit as I didn't want to disturb the surrounding classes with the sound of me pounding up the stairs. I slowed to a walk and Larry looked at me with a gigantic smile on his face, his gold teeth on prominent display, and said, "Hey, you can't be showing up late to class because that is going to affect your grade." I looked at him in disbelief as we both well knew that he, of all people, was never on time. I laughed and he laughed as well, but I kept on going right past him because I was not a 6'6" All Star and needed to get to class on time to keep my grades up.

Then there was Carlos Mendeguia, a high school friend from Carson City. Carlos was an almost mythical human creature in that he excelled at both sports and work. He was the youngest of four siblings and the only boy among three older sisters. Carlos's family owned a restaurant in Carson City called Toki Ona, which, in Basque, means "good place." His parents, Maria and Seruapio, had run it for years. His mother was in charge of all aspects of the restaurant: ordering supplies of meat, produce, and alcohol; scheduling and supervising all of the workers; and cooking all of the meat for the restaurant. Meanwhile, Mr. Mendeguia served as the bartender. To the common observer, one might think that he was not doing very much, other than serving drinks at the bar, but looks could be deceiving. Mr. Mendeguia would begin his shift as the bartender at 5:30 p.m. after his first job as a guard at the local prison, where he worked the 4:00 a.m. to 2:00 p.m. shift. In between jobs, he would go and attend to any issues pertaining to the twenty-unit mobile home complex that the family also owned. There were always issues with the trailers from sewer problems to lack of hot water to routine maintenance.

In addition to all these endeavors, the family also owned a feed store to supply feed for the livestock of local farmers. Carlos grew up working at Toki Ona's as far back as he could remember, where he served as the dishwasher seven days a week. His three older sisters were the servers for the restaurant. This was a family-run place and no one besides immediate family members worked there until Teresa, the youngest daughter, left for college. At that point, Carlos was promoted to server, and they hired a dishwasher to take over his duties. Carlos worked in the restaurant all during high school and served some pretty famous people including Clint Eastwood as well as Mike O'Callaghan, the former governor of Nevada, who came in every Sunday. In the summers, Carlos continued to work at his family's restaurant each night while also waiting tables in the morning at another restaurant, Harvey's. On his occasional days off, he would work at The Sizzler in nearby Tahoe. Simply put, Carlos's work ethic was unmatched. I observed his phenomenal work ethic from the sidelines for many years and it was clear that I needed to incorporate a bit of his tenacity into my own life.

CHAPTER THIRTY-THREE

I am nervously waiting in line to board the Hiller UH-12E helicopter. I silently watch as Spencer and Carlos clamber aboard the chopper, their gear slung securely over their shoulders, close the narrow door, are lifted into the sky, and quickly disappear behind Salmon Mountain.

After our sophomore year at UNLV, Spencer, Carlos, and I had gotten summer jobs on a "Silver State Hot Shot Crew," tasked with identifying and eradicating wildfires. We were spending our summer fighting fires to make money to pay for college tuition that coming fall. I was lucky to get one of the last spots on the crew thanks to Spencer, who put in a good word for me with Gary Johnson, an old hot shot who was now the supervisor in charge of hiring. I had traveled north from Las Vegas to Carson City with Gina to meet with him in person in the hopes of impressing him enough so that he would hire me. I met with Gary who asked just two questions during my interview: Will you work hard? And when can you start? I was thrilled to get the job and since Gary was such a nice person, I did not want to disappoint him.

* * *

I was left behind along the bottom of the Salmon River that divides Idaho and Montana. From this location, one could see Missoula off in the distance. The air was crisp and cool at 7:00 a.m. and a strong scent of pine wafted through the air from the evergreens that grew thickly along the river. The mild air was Mother Nature's ruse as the temperature would steadily and surely rise throughout the day. It was July and by midday, the temperature would be eighty degrees by the river and a scorching ninety-five degrees on the mountain.

The Hiller returned and it was now my turn to take a ride on "The Beast," my affectionate nickname for the helicopter. It looked like a giant insect as it was made almost entirely of glass and surrounded three seats. The glass began from behind the seats and enveloped the passengers as well as the pilot before coming together at the pilot's feet. Designed to maximize visibility, the helicopter allows passengers to see everything around and beneath them. Riding aloft the mountains in The Beast, you feel like you are floating on air, and it is used to explore the more difficult terrain here in Salmon, Idaho. However, I am not a fan of heights and I had been subjected to countless rides on other helicopters so far that summer during the height of the fire season. I had flown on a Bell UH-1Y helicopter several times earlier in the summer during other forest fires and I loathed the way the chopper bumped around in the air. So, the thought of riding on The Beast scared the hell out of me because it was so small and open.

Suddenly, I heard the sound of the blades twirling as they cut through the air. I looked up and saw the chopper cut the corner as it maneuvered expertly around the mountain. It was still loud even though I was wearing earplugs. As I watched it descend, I could literally see the blades crashing into the air. The copter got closer to the ground, and sand and dirt started to hit my face as The Beast created a small plume of air, dust, and dirt as it landed. A crew member known as the "hell-a-tack" looked directly at me and yelled, "Are you ready?"

I screamed, "Yes."

He nodded at me and then quickly warned me: "Remember to keep your head down as you board the helicopter." I had my fire helmet on, and I ducked to ensure that I literally kept my head on straight.

I boarded the chopper with Rigs, whose real name is Keller, the photographer for the crew. Rigs was thirty-five years old and in wildland firefighting, which is like being a senior citizen. A seasoned veteran, he had been on several fire crews in the past. After I boarded The Beast, I turned around and Rigs quickly snapped a picture of me smiling before we took off. As we lifted off the ground, I shook with terror because I detested flying on small aircraft above treacherous mountains and I always got queasy.

As we quickly climbed to 4,700 feet, the chopper tilted to the left and I could almost see over the pilot's head. The Salmon River glistened in the sun below us as we turned to climb another 4,000 feet. The Beast had no doors, in order to provide easy entry and exit for the crew, and I was sitting in the middle where it was very windy and loud. I had my headphones on so I could hear the pilot. He asked me, "Are you okay?"

"Yes," I responded, "but I don't like helicopters."

I immediately regretted saying that as he laughed and said, "Is that so?" He pushed the gearshift near my leg to the right and we quickly descended to 500 feet. I could now see over Rigs's head as I stared at the ground below. Rigs laughed as he enjoyed the pilot's little prank and I felt as if my stomach was still residing at 7,000 feet in the air. The pilot then pulled back on the gearshift and the helicopter zoomed off like a rocket as we hurtled straight up in the air. Rigs roared with excitement.

Finally, we leveled off at 12,000 feet and I looked down. All I could see was the fire raging all around, smoke billowing up as the fire ravaged the scrub brush and trees on the mountainside. The chopper dipped suddenly and raced around the fire line to the landing site. We were up in the mountains now, at an elevation of about 8,700 feet, when The Beast touched the ground. Over the next seven hellish days, we did our best to contain this seemingly never-ending, all-consuming fire.

After the fire was put out, we performed what was called "mop-up" duty, which entailed watching the smoldering fire and looking out for any burning embers. This particular fire had been burning high on the mountain and the Fire Service wanted to ensure that this one did not flame up again, so they commanded us to sit on this fire for longer than usual, three whole days under clear blue skies overlooking majestic mountains, deep-bottomed rivers, and glistening streams. Sitting there in the expansive outdoors felt like opening a door in your home and welcoming in the first spring air after a long, cold winter. I sat on the mountainside and contemplated my future.

* * *

Spending that summer working on a fire line as a member of a "hot-shot crew" was a hot, long way from normal society, but it also provided certain key lessons. For one thing, rigorous manual labor made me want something more out of life. But for another thing, we also spent hours looking over God's country. Big Sky country out in Montana is marked by big, bountiful, blue skies. The unexpected solitude of those days really got to me.

After one year at Mesa and one year at UNLV, I was entering my junior year of college and feeling the pressure to determine my future path. What did I want to be? I had been considering going to law school for some time, but still, I wondered, what did I really want to do with my life? Despite these concerns, my thoughts turned from my own career to personal fulfillment, and I was struck by a troubling thought: Was there more I could do to strengthen the relationships with those I cared the most about? Sure, I had friends and I had family, but was I really investing enough in those relationships? As I sat there under a cloudless sky looking over that mountain, I made a decision to tighten my relationships with the people I cared about the most and vowed to build stronger bonds with my friends.

As I looked out to the east, Carlos and Spencer sauntered over and sat down next to me and we spent the next few hours talking and gazing out over the mountains. As we sat on that hill, I knew my life was about to change again. I was not sure where it was going to go, but I knew it was going to be different. We continued to sit for a long time in the dirt on that hill until Carlos finally said, "We should get back to work and start looking for hot spots."

Eventually, we left that mountain and when we did I was determined to take a risk for my future. Instead of returning to Las Vegas, I decided to go back to San Diego and start my life again.

RENO

THE BIGGEST LITTLE CITY IN THE WORLD

Hotel
Goodbyes

CHAPTER THIRTY-FOUR

*A*fter that summer working for the Silver State Hot Shot Crew, and in preparation of my return to San Diego, I bought a 1976 tan Dodge Dart car from Mr. Hopper, my old baseball coach and the father of my boyhood friend and fellow rapper, Travis Hopper. Just as I was packing up my new car to return to San Diego, Kip Perry called me with the good news that his parents were going to let a group of us live in their house in San Diego. It was going to be me, Kip, and the two Johns, Sackett and Eck. Eventually, another high school friend—and another "John"— John Wurster, joined us as well. Now, I just needed to figure out what college I was going to attend in San Diego.

The Perry (a.k.a. "Pirazzi") house was a five-bedroom house also known as the "Grade Buster," for its tendency to lead its residents to poor grades. Naturally, Kip was the leader of the house. That fall, I moved into the Grade Buster house, started to look for jobs, and tried to figure out which college to attend. I had the grades to get into San

Diego State but I had my heart set on the University of San Diego. I had applied two times before, once after high school and once after one year at Mesa, and unfortunately turned down each time.

I was beginning to think they were never going to accept me. I needed to do something to make my application stand out, and I knew the best time to apply to colleges was for the spring semester since there is less competition than in the fall.

That fall, while I was getting my USD application together, I managed to get a job as a janitor at a local preschool working from 3:00 to 9:00 p.m. The preschool wanted someone with experience working as a janitor in a school district and who could pass a background check. I had worked for Mr. Courtright back in Carson City and I had a clean record, so I checked both boxes. It was tough to even get a job back then because the economy was not doing very well in 1991.

I was also excited to return to San Diego because I had met a girl named Fiona during my freshman year at Mesa, and we decided to see each other when I returned. I'd had a couple of girlfriends over the years such as one in high school who was very sweet and nice. However, I was not in a state to be a good or even decent boyfriend, so we broke up when we went to college. For many years, I was emotionally unavailable and not prepared to share my feelings with anyone else. I had way too many insecurities to be ready for vulnerability in a romantic relationship. Was it because of my past experiences? I don't know. Perhaps I was just a typical teenage boy. In any case, I didn't want to get serious with anyone in high school, and girls are generally more serious than boys about relationships at that age.

In college, you're encouraged to meet new people and participate in projects and opportunities that might be different from your past experience. And in my freshman year at Mesa, I met Fiona and was moved by her intelligence and her drive for something more. We were very different. She was from Connecticut, an English major, and very Catholic. She was also a perfectionist, and I was not. She was a follower of rules; I was not. She had parents that she was close to and wanted to please. I had a mom, too, and wanted to please her as well, but I had more flexibility to do what I wanted. Fiona was very nice, but also somewhat direct and had her own strong opinions. I could be more circumspect. We spent hours talking about politics, religion, and the direction of the country. She was always thinking of something bigger. She was the first person outside of my friends who I would turn to for advice or listen to for support. Eventually we broke up, but my development as a person would not have happened without Fiona, and we remained good friends. She told me truths that sometimes you can only hear in a relationship.

Fiona helped me with my third and final USD application essay. I also spoke to several admission officers and advisors at the college. It was going to be a long shot, so I decided that I needed someone who would vouch for me. I asked John Eck to write a letter of recommendation for me but felt vulnerable and embarrassed because I had no one else to turn to at this point. I think John was surprised as he didn't think a referral from him, a mere student, would carry much weight. I disagreed, and he finally agreed to write the letter.

I was so humbled. John had been hesitant because he wanted me to get in on my own merit. But he also knew that a helpful nudge might get my foot in the door. The rest was up to me. I was truly grateful and, in the spring of 1992, I was accepted at the University of San Diego.

RENO

THE BIGGEST LITTLE CITY IN THE WORLD

Hotel Goodbyes

CHAPTER THIRTY-FIVE

1994

SAN DIEGO, CALIFORNIA

At long last, it's graduation day from college. I slowly rise from the bed and walk over to wake my brother Dana, who is now nineteen years old. He is lying on the couch scrunched up in a ball. As I touch his shoulder, it feels as if we have traveled back in time to when I was nine and he was six and we were still living together, either in a motel room in Reno or in some foster home. *How many times had I woken him during my lifetime?* I look down at him, my closest biological sibling, from whom I was separated for too many years. He slowly turns over and opens his eyes. Dana has enormous, soulful brown eyes. Most folks don't think we're related because his eyes are so much bigger than mine.

"Wow," he says. "What time did we go to bed last night?"

"Late," I tell him. "You need to get a shower."

By the way Dana moves, slowly lifting his lanky 6'2" frame off the couch and edging up the stairs, I can tell he is hung over.

*   *   *

"It's time," a voice rings out in my head, and I look in the mirror one last time. I am clean shaven for this special day with a neatly trimmed goatee, a look I have been sporting for the past year. My friend Meng had come over a couple of days previously and trimmed my hair up nice for the event.

As I look in the mirror, I stare deep into my own eyes. All I see is light brown inside the whites of my eyes. The brim of my hat almost touches the mirror. *This tassel is going to bug me all day*, I think to myself, *but I will deal with it.* I adjust the white and blue collar around my neck, and it looks good. I did a surprisingly decent job ironing my graduation gown so it's smooth and unwrinkled.

I place my hands flat on the tile counter and breathe in and exhale slowly as if I am summoning an ancient spirit. I look down at the bathroom counter and I can feel the cold tile beneath both my hands. My head is tilted down as I ease my head up one more time to look in the mirror and see myself. Really see myself. I feel as if there is an emotional volcano in me about to explode. I am so filled with joy and excitement but also relief and sadness. I feel like I'm still a child. I watch as tears form in my eyes, unable to hold back my happiness and joy. So much belief in myself has finally come to fruition and so much pain has been shelved.

I am silent as the tears roll down my cheeks. My nose starts to water a bit as I allow this moment to happen. It's as if my old self is saying goodbye to my new self, but I don't see a twenty-three-year-old man in the mirror. Instead, I see that little boy in Ohio who believed that things would be all right although he had no evidence or proof at the time. That boy, who sat in the corner of a motel room for hours, days, without any stimulation or attention, waiting for his mother who never came. He lost his childhood at an early age and in exchange developed a deep-seated determination and belief in himself. I see him reaching out to me; that boy is saying goodbye to me.

I observe him deep behind my eyes. "I am so happy for you," he whispers as if he knew that I would make it all along. "Look at you," says the five-year-old boy to the grown man. "You did it!"

In the background, my friend Sackett is playing his favorite song by Big Head Todd and the Monsters called "Bittersweet." I have heard that song on countless occasions, but I never really listened to the lyrics before. The last part touches me:

I know we don't talk about it
We don't tell each other
All the little things that we need
We work our way around each other
As we tremble and we-
As we tremble and we bleed
As we tremble and we-
As we tremble and we bleed
It's bittersweet
More sweet than bitter
Bitter than sweet
It's a bittersweet surrender

"Thompson! Let's go!" John Wurster shouts, breaking my reverie as he wrangles everyone up for pictures. I wipe my eyes and smile one last time at him, the little boy inside of me. I know I cannot tap into his power anymore. He gave me all he had for the past seventeen years, and he surrendered it to me now. I open the door and say, "Here I come!"

* * *

It was a balmy seventy-six degrees on that June graduation day in San Diego. I sat in my chair and looked at the graduation speaker, waiting for him to call our names. I was eager to get this thing done with so we could get back to the Grade Buster house as Kip's dad was hosting a barbeque with a Mariachi band. After what seemed like an interminably long time, the names of the graduates began to be called.

There were about six hundred people in my graduating class at the University of San Diego. After two years, I was graduating with a major in political science and a minor in philosophy. I listened to the announcer and heard him call out, "William Brewer." There was a long way to go before my name was called. Unfortunately, I would not be graduating with honors; however, in my first semester at USD I made the dean's list with a 3.3 GPA and I would graduate with a 3.4 GPA in my major, political science, and a 3.6 GPA in my minor, philosophy, with an overall GPA of 2.98. Not bad for a child whose mom abandoned him at the age of nine.

I turned around, looked over my shoulder, and watched Dana and Gina from a distance. They knew each other quite well by this point, with Dana having visited me at my new home several times. They sat side by side in the hot sun—emblematic of my blended family. Gina had just graduated a week before from UNLV. Unfortunately, Kathy was not able to make the trip, but I know she was smiling for me at home.

I felt special but very ordinary. I had family in the stands, and I was eager to take the next steps in my life. I still could not believe it was actually happening. I was graduating from college that day. And not just any college, but a bona fide, highly acclaimed institution. The announcer read, "Joseph Temple." The students in our row stood up and began to walk forward. This was so different from high school. I knew very few people here in the stands and a small number of students in the chairs next to me. Unlike in high school, barely anyone knew my childhood or history. I began to feel hot as I stood fidgeting and waiting for my name to finally be called. I was just one person away from being called up on stage and butterflies began to flutter in my stomach. I quickly double checked my to-do list: Did I turn in all my assignments? Were there any outstanding parking tickets for me to pay? I was pretty sure that I took care of everything weeks ago, but I still wanted to be sure as USD was very strict when it comes to late fees. They would not hesitate to take this away from me right at the last moment. My thoughts were interrupted by the announcer calling out, "Stephen Jon Thompson."

I walked forward, shook the hand of the dean, and smiled for the photographer. Behind me, I heard faint applause and a few cheers. I turned and walked down the stage without any fanfare and took a seat in my original chair. "I did it," I said to myself. I really did.

CHAPTER THIRTY-SIX

*D*ana opened the door of my silver Mitsubishi Montero and climbed in as we took off down Highway 50 toward Sacramento. He had just finished his day shift at the Horizon Casino, and I'd gotten the day off from my job as a blackjack dealer at Harrah's Casino in Lake Tahoe. My friend Carlos and I had always talked about working as blackjack dealers after college before embarking on a more serious career. We both went to blackjack school and landed jobs at Harrah's. It was also nice to be living and working near Dana.

It was a hot summer evening in Lake Tahoe and the air, rich with the scent of pine, was still. I turned onto Pioneer Trail Road like I had done countless times before. However, this trip was different. Dana and I were heading back to Sacramento, but not sharing a seat, hungry and ticketless on a Greyhound bus. We were in a car, one that I bought with my hard-earned cash from my job as a blackjack dealer. I was twenty-four, Dana twenty-one, and the day had come that after fifteen years, we were going to see our younger siblings again, Eugene, Brian, and Tierra.

I had been trying to find the three little ones ever since I graduated from college. I knew that not long after I'd arrived at the children's home, Gus had collected the three of them and taken them back to Sacramento. But now, a decade later, I had no idea where to start looking, so all I could do was search the internet, which, because it had limited information at the time, was pretty discouraging. But then Dana mentioned to me that an old high school girlfriend had heard of Eugene, and that his foster mother Marjorie knew where they were. After one phone call, Dana had their address and confirmation that they wanted to see us as well. They were just two hours away. I was daunted. I felt as if I was stepping back in time, but I was excited to see my brothers and sister.

"It's going to be strange," I said to Dana.

"I know," he said. "Maybe they won't remember us."

"I wonder if Gus will be there?" I asked.

Did I want to see Gus? Not really. Was he going to be the same asshole I'd seen fifteen years before? I was apprehensive.

After two hours, we pulled onto Watt Avenue, Sacramento. The neighborhood was run-down, and the houses looked unkempt with weeds, couches, and cars littering the yards. We parked next to a white Cadillac outside a house that was surrounded by a chain-link fence. Its outer walls were dull, in need of paint, and the front door was wide open in an attempt to let some cooler air inside. Through the screen, I could see that the house was dark inside. I looked down for a moment to switch off the engine, took a deep breath, and turned to Dana.

"Here we go," I said.

Then, as I turned to open the car door, I saw a 6'6", 260-pound Black man standing in the doorway. I was taken aback by how his body filled the entire frame. He was dark and bald with a whitish scar on his bottom lip. His arms were crossed firmly across his chest, and he glared menacingly at the world, as if expecting an intruder. It was my little brother Eugene. When I last laid eyes on him, he was a cowering and unsure four-year-old boy, all sinew and bone. But now, he was huge. But I would have recognized Eugene anywhere. I looked at Dana and he grinned at me.

As we approached Eugene, he broke into a wide smile and my heart almost burst with joy. He gave Dana a big hug, and then enveloped me with his huge arms. I breathed him in, felt his size, squeezed him to me. He was no longer a little one for me to protect and guide.

As we followed Eugene into the house, I was thrown back to the years I spent with Brenda and Gus moving in and out of ramshackle rental homes and motels. Was I going to see the man that had starved me and dangled me over a balcony by my ankle? My eyes adjusted to the dark and then I saw Brian. I tried to read him. He seemed more reserved than Eugene and clearly didn't remember me. But I knew it was him, so I walked toward him. "Hey," I said and put my arms around him. He hugged me back.

I felt the world slow down around me. I knew these people. They were my flesh and blood, but at the same time I couldn't quite comprehend what was happening. I was glad that Dana was very much taking the lead.

And then, I saw him. I'd told Dana on the way down that if Gus said anything out of line, I wasn't going to take his bullshit. And here he was—my old tormentor flashing his trademark smile at me.

"Hey," I said.

"You were that badass kid when you were younger," said Gus.

A badass kid? Was this some kind of half-assed compliment referring to my determination to stay alive or was he trying to make some excuse for being a total shit to me because I was a bad kid? Either way, Gus was trying to manipulate me as usual. But the power he'd once had over me was gone. He was short and old and bald. I just smiled. Dana hugged Gus. I looked at Eugene, who was still smiling. But I sensed that Brian wasn't comfortable around Gus.

A car door slammed, and Eugene yelled, "Tierra come on in here. Your older brothers are here." A young woman came through the door.

My baby sister, Tierra. How many times did I carry this young woman on my hip and rock her to sleep? My heart swelled. She looked at me and Dana. I could tell that she didn't want a hug.

"Hey, it's good to see you," I said.

We perched on the edge of the couches. Gus wandered in and out as we chatted about work and where we were living. Brian and Tierra complimented me on my car.

"Can I drive it?" Tierra asked.

"Do you have a license?" I asked her.

"No," she responded.

"I do," said Brian.

I threw him the keys and watched the pair of them run excitedly outside, leaving Dana and me with Eugene to talk. When Brian and Tierra came back about fifteen minutes later, we talked some more, and then the five of us went out for food. I felt more relaxed to be away from Gus. We spent the time learning about each other and eventually I plucked up the courage to ask if any of them had seen Brenda.

"She died," Eugene said.

I felt nothing.

"When did you see her last?" asked Dana.

"Last year," responded Eugene.

Dana and I dropped our siblings back at their house and promised to keep in touch with them. It was a long drive back to Tahoe. We were heavy with the realization that both Dana and I had many opportunities that our siblings had not been given. Maybe Brenda really had hoped that foster care would lead us to a life she could never give us. And maybe that had worked out for Dana and me. It was a lot to absorb in one day.

CHAPTER THIRTY-SEVEN

That summer of 1995, when I met my siblings again, I was twenty-four years old—the age for going out partying, meeting girls, drinking, gambling, and betting on sports. It was a great time and even though I was back in the casino environment, I wasn't plagued by the memories of my childhood. Brenda popped into my mind a few times a year but only if someone found out I was adopted and asked me where my real mom was.

The casino job was meant to be temporary. I still firmly planned on going to law school. I thought studying law would be a good way to do something and make a difference in people's lives. And if you want to go into politics, the law is a logical path. Many US congressmen and most US presidents have been lawyers. I had taken the LSAT the summer after I graduated from college, but I had failed to get a score that could even get me into Jerry's Law School—diner by day, law school by night. I always thought that I would attend, but it never happened.

My passion for politics was further cemented by working as an attaché, or secretary, for the Nevada State Assembly in early 1996. I worked with Mark Manendo and Saundra (Sandi) Krenzer, who were both Democrats. I didn't necessarily enjoy all the paperwork and research I had to do, but I loved being on the floor, hearing the debates, and working with the lobbyists.

Later that same year, I went back to Tahoe, working first at Bill's Casino, owned by Harrah's Lake Tahoe, then at Harrah's Lake Tahoe, where I was a shift supervisor. When I became a beverage shift supervisor, I managed a team. It was a great opportunity as we had a huge budget and hundreds of employees. It was another opportunity for me to observe people, both employees and customers, and how to interact with them when they're losing and when they're winning. But I still had bigger plans than just working in a casino.

While working as an attaché at the Nevada State Assembly, I had met politicians such as Dean Heller, who later became a US senator, and Brian Sandoval, who was then the governor of Nevada. I was also friends with Steven Horsford, the first African American to serve as majority leader in the state senate. The timing seemed perfect for me to make a run for Nevada State Assembly, District 40, which was my home district in Carson City. I wanted to give back to the community that had given me so much.

I was the Democratic candidate running against Mark Amodei, a Republican lawyer and Native Nevadan from Carson City. The issue that really had me fired up was public transportation. Carson didn't have a bus service, which disproportionately affected the young, the old, and the poor. I campaigned on this issue and on increasing vocational education programs for kids who weren't going to go to college.

By this time, I'd met Penelope Hatfield. We had first met at blackjack school in Lake Tahoe. Penelope was a bright light, young, happy to take on the world, with an inner confidence. She was also stable and well-balanced. This suited me because I didn't want to be anyone's emotional dialysis machine. Not that I necessarily thought of it that way at the time, I just thought Penelope was beautiful and wanted to hang out with her. But there are reasons we're attracted to certain people, and I think this is one of the things that was appealing about Penelope. Given everything that had happened to me, I could have become extremely needy and dependent, or jealous and controlling, but I'd gone the other way. I didn't want to consume anyone, and I didn't want them to consume me either. In college, I took a class called Philosophy of Love. This helped me to see that love didn't need to be perfect and that two people didn't have to be the entire world to each other. It made sense to me because I had witnessed and experienced such catastrophic love up to that point. To open myself up to love only if it was perfect and flawless would have made me far too vulnerable. I had been afraid to be vulnerable in relationships, but Penelope started to change that.

She was also very supportive of my political ambitions. I decided to put together a political commercial for local television, which no one was really doing at the time. It was cheap because political ads were subsidized, and I had the choice to do either a video or a series of photographs accompanied by a voiceover. I preferred to use some photographs, but there was a problem: I had barely any photographs of myself. Just a few from high school and from firefighting with the Silver State Hot Shot Crew. So, I decided to go and look for my file in the Nevada state archives in Carson City. My mom Kathy had mentioned it to me many times over the years, but I'd never made the effort.

A couple of days later, Penelope and I went to the Nevada state library, Archives and Public Records division. It was easy to find since it was near my old home, the Northern Nevada Children's Home. It was a strange experience to walk into an institution to find information about myself. I anticipated receiving large folders with tons of items attached. I had worked at the Nevada State Assembly and was used to getting documents from the archives. Generally, there was so much stuff that it came in boxes. To my surprise, after I showed my ID, they handed me a single yellow legal-size envelope. That's all there was on Stephen Jon Thompson.

But what I found in my file was fascinating. There were pictures of me on field trips and church trips. But I was more interested in other things, like what was being said about my behavior and progress from my counselors, social workers, or teachers, or whether anyone from the state had been able to reach members of my family. What Penelope found moving were the images of people taking care of me. We never used any of those photographs in a political commercial, but it offered me a fascinating window into my early life.

At first, I thought running for office was a good first step in my political career, but then I started to think that maybe I could win and make a real impact on the community. People couldn't believe what I was doing, especially with the potential of losing and losing badly, but as usual I felt that I had nothing to lose. I had a lot of support too. Kathy and Penelope went out and campaigned on my behalf.

I ended up losing the election by a respectable margin: Amodei's 5,759 votes to Thompson's 3,935. My opponent had outspent me 8 to 1 and, of course, he was an elected official. Although I lost the election by almost 20 percent, it was a presidential election year and I received more votes than the incumbent Democratic President Bill Clinton in my district, which was 68 percent Republican and 35 percent Democrat. The fact that we raised $40,000 for my first campaign, and that we could do well on a limited budget, was impressive to many. Additionally, my opponent was twelve years older and a far more established politician. I felt fine about the loss. I did my best and it was an incredible experience to meet so many great people in Carson City and across the great state of Nevada.

Today, Mark Amodei is a US congressman, the only Republican in the Nevada congressional delegation. I saw him a few years back at a fundraiser for the Nevada Military Support Alliance, and I think he always respected how well I had done in the race. After my stab at politics, I moved to the Bay Area and began the path that led me to where I am today.

* * *

Penelope knew about my past quite early on in our relationship. I explained that I had lived in a group home and been adopted by Kathy. By some miracle, I had found someone not only compassionate but also extremely emotionally intelligent. I didn't really trust love at that time. I do now. I found Penelope, a woman who wanted her own space and who gave me the space to be me too. I want her to expand and grow, and I guess that's how I want to be treated too.

After two decades together, Penelope has observed the ways in which the past remains with me. For many years I had abandonment issues. I would dream that she had left me, and then take it up with her the next day as if it had actually happened. She still tends to stay physically far away from me when waking me up in the morning as I leap out of bed very aggressively. Ready for what, I don't know. Maybe to save Brenda from a maniac with a bat or perhaps ready to appease Uncle Eugene and shepherd my siblings to safety in the middle of the night. To wake me, Penelope usually goes to the edge of the room, turns the light on, and calls out my name.

I'm generally the cook in the house but if Penelope cooks, she always makes enough so that I can have seconds. I need to know there is enough food. She learned to serve me a smaller portion to start with, so that I always knew there was more to eat. And the heat! If Penelope's cold, she puts on a sweater. But I'll say, "No. I don't want to be cold. We can afford the heat. We're putting the heat on!" I am no longer that freezing cold little boy sleeping in a car on Christmas Eve. I decided early on that I would have my own home, enough food to eat, and, of course, heat.

Although I'm sure I can be infuriating to Penelope at times, she is very patient and a great listener. She slows me down as I tend to both think and move way too fast at times. I don't explain things very well. I connect a lot of dots but I'm also happy to relax with ambiguity. She's really figured out how to deal with me. She once told me, "I would never ask you more than two questions in a row because I know that after the second one, I've lost you." Penelope might ask, "What are we having for dinner?" and "Did you take out the trash?" But by the third question, I feel there are too many demands being made on me, that I'm being managed or limited. I'm not of course, but those are the buttons it presses. It takes me right back to being a powerless little boy at the whims of Brenda, or under the watchful eye of Lee Wilhelm, constrained by the expectations that people place on a Black kid from a children's home.

CHAPTER THIRTY-EIGHT

2016
BOSTON, MASSACHUSETTS

*I*leave the cobblestoned streets of Manhattan's Meatpacking District and head north to Penn Station. It's 7:00 a.m. on a Friday at the end of November and the streets are cold, quiet, and littered with the final few leaves of fall. A few cars honk their horns as people scurry to hail cabs or head down into the subway. It's not quite winter but given the unseasonably cold weather I am wrapped in a scarf and gloves. I had to buy them when leaving work at the Empire State Building a few days previously. My work with the tech company LinkedIn in the city done, I'm to catch the 8:03 a.m. Amtrak to Boston to visit my Aunt Ouida.

Boston is her birthplace, and she has returned there in her later years. I am pleased to be visiting her after so many years. I am now in my midforties. I stow my bags in the overhead luggage bin and sit down ready to trek 224 miles north. I will have over three hours to think about Brenda's younger sister. She and I had made contact a few weeks previously after another sibling of hers contacted me via Facebook. Ouida was the family member I was closest to, and I wanted to connect with her and maybe get some more information about my mother. The last time I saw Aunt Ouida was through the back windshield of her husband Jerry's car as it pulled out of her Youngstown driveway carrying Brenda's then partner Gus, myself, and my younger brother Dana off into the night. At the time, I was seven and Dana was five. It has been thirty-seven years since we left her warm and loving home.

It seems as if my aunt, now almost sixty and no longer with Jerry, is the glue that has held the family together for so many years. She is a loving and caring person, reflected best by the fact that at the young age of nineteen she asked Social Services if she could have Dana and me live with her and Jerry. I didn't have my first child until I was in my thirties, so it's hard for me to understand how she willingly took responsibility for Dana and myself at such a young age. But she did it and provided us with a stable and secure home, albeit too briefly, as well as a sense of normalcy against the traumatic backdrop of our early lives.

As far as anyone looking at me on this Amtrak train can tell, I am a regular everyday guy. What they might not know is that I've worked at private companies trying to go public and Fortune 10 companies that you use every day, such as LinkedIn, Apple, and Google. I founded my own recruiting company in 1998 when I was twenty-eight years old after graduating from a good university. Currently, I am a successful professional in the software industry where I work for a Fortune 500 company and earn a good living. As an executive recruiter, I spend my days searching for and hiring some of the smartest and most unique people in the world. I live in a million-dollar home in San Jose and own several investment properties around California. I serve as a board member at a nonprofit environmental organization that protects the San Francisco Bay. I have a wonderful family consisting of two funny and talented children, a host of siblings, and extended relatives, including a family descended from Mexican immigrants who opened their home and hearts to me as my foster mom and sister many years ago. Finally, I have an amazing wife who supports me through thick and thin.

As the train lurches forward, its rhythmic chugging lulling the passengers to settle into their seats, we travel underground then slowly rise above to the surface, the sun glinting off the skyscrapers, bright against the luminous blue sky. I sip my coffee and watch the tenements and office buildings speed past as I consider how it will be to see my aunt after almost four decades. Will I be nervous? Will I be emotional seeing someone who nurtured me during my often-perilous childhood? I close my eyes and drift away. An image of my nine-year-old self emerges…

* * *

When I saw my Aunt Ouida bundled up in her winter clothes beneath the giant station clock in the South Station train terminal, I recognized her instantly. She looked at me as I walked toward her, then when I was close enough, she pulled me into a hug saying, "Oh my God. You look just like your mom."

I hugged her back, then she pulled away to admire me and said, "You're so tall," as people do when they have not seen a niece or a nephew in years. It was good to see her. We walked to a restaurant to grab lunch and spend some time catching up.

After several hours of talking and reminiscing, Aunt Ouida sighed and said, "Well, Stephen, you have done really well for yourself. I see you took advantage of the opportunities that were given to you. I wish I had done more to take advantage of my opportunities when they arose in my life."

I didn't say anything, but I understood what she meant. Later that night, after we'd parted ways with hugs and kisses and promises of keeping in touch, I found myself ruminating on what she had said. She was right. For me, the unplanned gift of Brenda's abandonment was a pivotal break in the cycle of substance abuse, poverty, and unplanned pregnancies. My aunt had a baby at a young age. Her parents were already dead, and she had no close family to support her. Then, aged only nineteen, she volunteered to take care of me and Dana and treated us as her own. We became her responsibility for nine months and even though we were ecstatic to be with our aunt, I'm sure that she desired more out of her life than simply caring for other people's children. She might have seen opportunities to advance her career and life, but by the time we left her she had one small baby and another one on the way. I couldn't help wondering how my life might have been so different if I had actually stayed with her.

As I sat listening to Aunt Ouida, my mind turned to the cycle of unplanned pregnancy that has plagued generations of my family and played no small part in the impoverishment, abuse, and despair that has marked us all, most significantly, the women and the children. Ouida, with only two children of her own, is the outlier among her sisters. Linda had four children with several fathers; Frieda had six children with several men; and Brenda, as we know, had seven children with five different men.

Several times during our conversation, Ouida proclaimed that she "did not need to have more children" as she spent a good part of her young adulthood caring for the offspring of her sisters. Looking back on it, one cannot help but notice a trend in my family, a trend that afflicts many young women in our country—namely, the burden of unplanned pregnancy. According to a recent *New York Times* article, nearly half of all pregnancies in the United States are unintended, with the majority of those pregnancies impacting women of color and working-class women.[1] These are women who are already facing extreme financial and cultural hardships. I witnessed firsthand the burden of having children at an extremely young age and the toll that it took not only on Brenda but on myself and my younger siblings.

Because she was saddled with all these young children with no father in sight, Brenda fell further into poverty, unable to provide for herself and her family. That free fall into economic disparity presumably played a large part in the less than stellar choices she made for herself, and the dangerous predicaments into which she placed herself and her children—associating with drug dealers, exposing her young children to drug paraphernalia and violence, prostituting herself to abusive men, and living in precarious situations in which our basic needs were barely or rarely met. The financial, emotional, and psychological demands that five young children place on any parent can be difficult to handle, but with financial means and a good support network, two parents can raise those children successfully.

Brenda had neither access to financial security nor the support of a stable network of family and friends to assist her with the enormous challenges that the five of us presented to her. As a result, she sank further into impoverishment and got sucked down by a daily wave of despair. She had no options to improve her life, and without a father or a steady male role model in our lives, we were pawns to Brenda's whims, ever more so given her proclivity to drink and take drugs. At

---

1   Claire Cain Miller, "More U.S. Women Are Avoiding Unwanted or Mistimed Pregnancies," *The New York Times*, May 3, 2023, https://www.nytimes.com/2023/05/03/upshot/pregnancy-birth-timing-preference.html.

moments, she tried to improve her life and attempted steady work, but with no more than a high school diploma, there was little hope for her to raise herself out of poverty working minimum-wage jobs at the local supermarket.

Hearing Ouida talk about my numerous nieces, nephews, aunts, and uncles, I was overwhelmed by the epidemic of fatherlessness that has plagued my family. Where were all the fathers? Ouida's own daughter, Sherri, was living with her in Boston and had a child of her own named Jada, but there was no father around. Despite that, Jada was recently accepted into a prestigious private school in Brookline, Massachusetts, and spends her summers at academic camps and her Saturdays with Latin tutors. At least Jada seems to be poised to break the cycle of poverty and unplanned pregnancies given the trajectory she has been placed on due to her intelligence and hard work.

After my conversation with my aunt, I felt overwhelmingly grateful. It was so great to see her after so many years. It was important for me to learn more about my grandmother Nana and her mother, my great grandmother, whom I never met.

I've never had the privilege of learning about the history of my grandparents as most children do. Establishing ties to family history is important to me and my siblings since we never had access to that information. I listened attentively to my aunt as she shared stories of her mother and siblings. It was inspiring to hear about people that shared my lineage. My aunt even told me about our Native American blood as our Oklahoma ancestors were members of the Choctaw tribe. I was not shocked as my grandmother Nana and my Aunt Ouida were so light-skinned in appearance, and it also explains why I have such admiration for Native American culture and people.

However, maybe the real culprit in this story is substance abuse. It was oddly comforting to know that I had not been crazy all these years when I spoke of my mother's profound drug and alcohol addictions. My aunt testified to the endemic alcohol abuse that runs through my family from Brenda to Nana and possibly even further back in time. As Ouida made clear, my mother came from a long-established line of drinkers and substance abusers.

Although I had not seen my aunt in over thirty-seven years, I felt at home with her almost instantly. I did not try to guard my comments and interactions. I was myself and it was truly enjoyable to be in her presence. I wish my brother Dana could have been there to hear the stories of my aunt and learn about her daughter and granddaughter. After what must have been a hard life, things seem to be going in the right direction for my Aunt Ouida, for which I was grateful. But my emotional attachment to her was nowhere near as strong as it had been when I was a young boy left in her care. She tried to do the best she could for me and that is something that I know with all my heart and being. However, I remained surprisingly emotionally unmoved during my visit with her. Those years spent in turmoil seem so far away, as do the tears I shed as I cried myself to sleep on countless nights. I no longer hold that pain close to the surface, and I have come to terms with my unconventional family history.

In a way, my aunt represents the last chapter in my family saga as she is the closest living person to Brenda. Given Brenda's early death, precluding my chance for any closure with her, Ouida, given her lineal proximity to my mother and the fact that she cared for me as a young child, was the next best thing. On some level, I was hoping that Ouida could provide the key to many of the questions that still linger for me regarding my mother and the choices she made. I had hoped that she might be able to fill in some of the hazy details of Brenda's early life and provide some insight into how we ended up where we did in that run-down motel room in Reno on that fateful day. Unfortunately, that was not to be the case since Ouida knew little about Brenda as the two sisters did not keep in close contact—perhaps by Brenda's design—and had a falling out several years before Brenda died. While my siblings have certainly helped fill in some of the gaps and provided explanations, in some ways, I feel that I am no closer now to knowing Brenda's exact reasons for abandoning us or why she never sought us out later in her life.

Closure, it seems, is not fated to be mine. Still, I walked away from my time with Aunt Ouida with a profound sense of gratitude. In the end, my family is not in Boston. Yes, my aunt resides there, and I will always cherish her, and I hope and know that I will continue to build our relationship into the future. And yet, like any adoptive child, I am more endeared to the family that raised and provided for me.

When I spoke to my aunt, I referred to Brenda, her sister and my biological mother, as "Brenda," not "mom." Yet, I referred to my adoptive mother, Kathy, as "my mom." A look of surprise registered in my aunt's eyes when I first said this, although she did not make any comment. But Brenda lost that title to me and my siblings years ago in that motel room. My siblings and I gave that deed to others who hold the title to our hearts as true mothers regardless of biology. Again, I am grateful. I am grateful because my birth mother gave me life and the discipline to be successful in life. All I am and will be comes from that fact, and my family has evolved to include new members and siblings now.

CHAPTER THIRTY-NINE

2023
SAN JOSE, CALIFORNIA

Over the years, I have learned from my siblings what happened to them over those long years we were separated. Back when all of us were fostered by Marjorie and Katie, Brian, who was only four, lived with two other boys and had a pretty rough time of it. They bullied Brian, made him eat dog food, and even whipped him on his hands with rulers and horse whips. A social worker would come by occasionally and at some point, after Dana and I had left the foster home, Brian told the social worker what was happening. She was moved to tears and promised to find Gus and sure enough, Gus collected Brian, Tierra, and Eugene and took them to Reno to live with him and his latest wife, Edna.

"Gus loved three things: women, alcohol, and fights," Brian told me. "He was always inviting people over, able to make friends wherever he went." But Brian, Eugene, and Tierra soon found out that it was not good to have people over because then Gus would get drunk and soon be gunning for a fight, sometimes with his own children. Brian quickly learned to fall to the ground on the first slap so he wouldn't suffer any more blows. Gus would also humiliate and threaten Brian. In one fit of rage, he vowed to knock Brian's head off his shoulders, dribble it around, and throw it through the basketball hoop. It seemed like much of the rage that Gus vented toward me turned to Brian after I departed.

Brian was three when Brenda abandoned us in the motel and didn't remember it at all. It was Gus's sister Shirley who relayed the whole story to Brian when he was in the eighth grade. Brian was totally shocked. Gus was getting divorced at the time, which is why the children were staying with Shirley. When Gus got a new place in a subdivision in Sacramento, Brian, Eugene, and Tierra moved back in with him and remained there through high school. Gus was on disability as he had gotten hurt in the military, and once again had remarried, this time to a woman named Linda. But that marriage too dissolved, and he later married Sandra.

I don't forgive Gus for what he did to me, but I can see that there might have been some circumstances that contributed to his behavior. He was a veteran of the Vietnam War and was medically discharged. Was he drinking to numb the pain or the mental trauma of war? Did he come home addicted to heroin, amphetamines, or sedatives like many other servicemen? Did he then get Brenda into drugs? None of this excuses his physical and emotional violence toward us kids, but it might at least explain it.

Brian told me that as far as Gus was concerned, Brenda was a nonentity. He never spoke about her. But then one incredible day, Gus was driving Brian and Tierra through Sacramento. They were moving to a new house for what seemed like the hundredth time when they stopped by a community center and Gus smiled at an attractive Black woman across the street. There he goes again, thought Brian, "hello ladies" mode. Gus pulled the truck over to the curb in front of the woman, let out a low whistle, and said, "Hey, girl. You lookin' good." The woman looked down at her feet, seemingly frozen to the sidewalk. "Whatcha doing 'round here?" Gus asked.

"Nothin'. Heading to work," she replied.

Brian and Tierra were bored by the whole encounter and their dad's attempts to gain female attention. Gus indicated the two children sitting in the car.

"You want me to tell them who you are?" he asked, giving a little chuckle. At that, Brian and Tierra started to take an interest.

"Naw. Naw," said the woman.

"C'mon, now. Don'tcha think they might wanna know?" Gus continued.

"Gus, I told you. No," the woman said. "Now stop it."

"All right, all right. Calm down. I ain't gonna give away your dark secrets."

Then he turned to Brian and Tierra and gestured to each of them as he introduced them: "This here is my son, Brian, and that over there is my daughter, Tierra."

The woman put out her hand as if to shake theirs and then abruptly pulled it away.

"Nice to meet you," she mumbled, looking at them with tears shining in her eyes. "You all look like real nice children. Real nice children."

She patted the windowsill of the truck door. "They is," said Gus. "They's mine, right?" He laughed. The woman nodded. There was an awkward silence for a minute as Brian and Tierra stared wide-eyed at the hunched over, sad woman standing on the sidewalk. Finally, Gus cleared his throat and said, "I tell ya what. Why don'tcha give me your phone number and maybe we can set something up. That work for you?"

The woman continued to nod as tears silently rolled down her cheeks. Gus took out a scrap of paper and a pen and jotted down his phone number. He then passed the piece of paper to the woman and waited as she quickly scrawled down her number with one hand, wiping her tears with the other. Then she slowly handed the paper back to Gus.

"Well, you take care of yourself, now," Gus said to the woman. She stood still and nodded again, watching as the truck pulled away, staring as Brian and Tierra watched out of the back windshield. As the car made a sharp left turn, Brian managed a half-hearted wave, but the woman had disappeared from view.

A few days later, Gus informed Brian that the woman they had met on the street was actually their mother, Brenda, and that Tierra was going to spend the summer with her in Salinas, California. Tierra did go and spend the summer with Brenda, returning home in the fall with the news that Brenda now had two other daughters with two different men.

A few years after that, Brian was in college and came home one day to find the house a wreck with stuff strewn everywhere and furniture overturned. Gus had been sent to jail. After he was released, he moved to Fresno for a short while, then to Ohio where he gave his life over to God, working as an ordained minister. Brian visited him many times out there, noting the overwhelming change that had taken place in Gus. He even had stopped drinking, a life-altering change. Apparently, Gus's last stint in jail had impacted him so much that it finally motivated him to change his ways, hence his involvement with the church. Once he was in Ohio, however, Gus suffered from health problems related to diabetes.

One day, as Brian was talking on the phone with Gus, he suddenly put his wife on, insisting that she had something important to tell

Brian. "Hello, Brian," she began. "You know … your dad loves you. He really loves you," after which she handed the phone back to Gus who continued the conversation as if nothing had been said. Brian was taken aback as Gus had never told his kids that he loved them. Apparently, Gus was well aware of how sick he was and wanted to get right with God. He died in 2005 at the age of fifty-seven.

Like many of my siblings, Brian harbored deep anger toward Gus for a long time. However, Gus's change helped Brian get over his anger and when Brian visited him in Ohio during the last years of his life, he realized that his father was a loving person, albeit one with a nasty drinking habit. Despite the pain that Gus had caused, Brian acknowledges that there were moments when he was a good father. Gus did try to provide for his kids as best he could.

Years later, reflecting on my relationship with Gus, I had to admit that for all he'd done to me, at least Dana had fonder memories of Gus, as did his biological children: Eugene, Brian, and Tierra. Whatever his failings, Gus still went back to get his kids when they were placed in foster care, unlike Brenda. His kids, ultimately, were extremely important to him even if he was not able to parent them lovingly and properly.

Brian's painful childhood caused him a great many struggles and by the time he reached eighth grade, he had been jailed for assault. He started a gang whose trademark was punching random people in the face. By ninth grade, he was routinely breaking into people's homes, stealing things, and selling drugs. At that point, he was arrested again, which proved to be a blessing in disguise as he met Donald North-cross, a deputy sheriff, who went to court to testify on his behalf. He became Brian's mentor through the Our Kids (OK) program that he had founded to help at-risk Black male youths. The judge recommended that Brian begin playing a sport to keep him out of further trouble and stipulated that Brian needed to remain in Northcross's care as part of the OK program.

In tenth grade, Brian began playing football and after graduating from high school, he attended community college in Salinas where he continued the sport and earned a scholarship to West Virginia Tech. He graduated from there with a degree in public administration followed by a master's degree in athletic administration from the University of West Virginia. He began his postcollege career working in West Virginia for the Upward Bound program. Northcross, his old mentor, then alerted him to a position at an Upward Bound program in Arkansas, where he worked his way up through several administrative positions to ultimately become the dean of Student Affairs at Arkansas Baptist College.

For her part, Tierra was also very close to Gus. When she was sixteen years old, Tierra had a daughter of her own, Taysha, and was very diligent in taking care of her. Perhaps due to Brenda's abandonment, Tierra was extremely protective of her own daughter and monitored her every move. She knew where she was every day before and after school. She walked her to the bus stop every day from grade school through her senior year of high school. Tierra worked hard to ensure that Taysha got everything she needed. She emphasized to her the importance of education and was determined that her daughter would graduate from high school and go on to college. Taysha recently graduated from high school with a 3.3 GPA and was accepted to Spelman College in Atlanta.

Brenda had told Gus that Eugene was his child but doubts always lingered. Gus, however, treated Eugene as his own, taking him in, admittedly into a far from perfect situation. Given his athletic prowess and physical strength, Eugene could very well have enjoyed an athletic career and most certainly a college scholarship. However, he was caught up being the protector and leader of his younger siblings. Unable to resist the lure of the streets, Eugene took to selling drugs, moving in and out of jail for various offenses. He has seen a lot of things that the rest of us have not but possesses grit and an unshakable inner confidence.

* * *

I'm not sure why it took him so long to tell me, but about five years ago, Dana told me that his foster mom had been a nurse at Washoe Medical Hospital in Reno and that one night, Brenda came into the hospital to deliver a child, a daughter named Charlene. Three years later, she had another daughter, Kendra. Charlene lives on the East Coast and has four children. Kendra and I met in 2003 at Eugene's house in Sacramento. She was fourteen at the time and eighteen years younger than me. Kendra says she was thirteen when she received a letter from Social Services saying her older brother was looking for her.

I gave her a lift home that day and she opened up about Brenda. "When my sister and I were small," Kendra said, "Mom sat us down and showed us this Filofax, an old address book. She said, 'If anything ever happens to me, in here, you'll find Gus. Gus and I have five other children. Gus will help you find them.'"

"What else did she tell you?" I asked.

"She said she'd left you in the motel room because she was in an abusive relationship with Gus, and she couldn't look after herself and she couldn't look after you. She was really chewed up about it, like heartbroken. It was hard for Charlene and me to understand that we had four brothers and a sister. Brenda was plagued by it. She knew she was sick, but she waited until the last possible minute until she went to hospital because I think she wanted to die. As she was being put in the ambulance, she told me she'd be okay, and we should go to school. But she never came home. That is the last memory I have of her."

Kendra also told me that Brenda would often tell her and Charlene, "Always take care of your kids." Charlene was eleven when her mother died, and Kendra was just eight. I was stunned. For so many years, I hadn't known about my mother's death, but now I know. She had died alone.

*   *   *

Over the past few years, Kendra has spent weekends and holidays with me and my family. The more she ages, the more she resembles Brenda in skin tone, hair color, and even her voice. It's strange that I'm the oldest and she's the youngest of the siblings, yet we are the most similar to each other and the two that most closely resemble Brenda. I feel close to Kendra, possibly because we both lost Brenda at a similar age. It's not easy to explain the bond that exists between all of us, separated though we were for so many years. Brenda connects us all. She is the thread that binds us, weaving together the myriad strands of all of our lives into a tightly woven fabric that reveals the scars that she left behind.

Recently, we all gathered at my vacation home in Discovery Bay, California, to host somewhat of a reunion for all of us siblings. Everyone was present except Charlene, who could not attend but was there in spirit. We also invited AB and Crystal, Gus's children from a relationship before Brenda. Our house teemed with cousins and children and siblings, and our collective roar echoed across the lake. I've never been with so many folks who looked like me, uttered the same sounds as me, and were as funny and zany and complex as me. We ended the day sitting on the deck watching the sunset as we swapped stories about Brenda and Gus while the fiery orange sun slowly sunk into the golden bay.

RENO
THE BIGGEST LITTLE CITY IN THE WORLD

Hotel
Goodbyes

CHAPTER FORTY

Growing up, I was the beneficiary of strong-willed women, for good or for bad—Brenda, Ouida, and Kathy. Brenda, my primary role model, was a strong Black woman, not one to mess with. Ouida, though barely out of high school, dug down and cared for Dana and me when no one else in our family could. Finally, my mother Kathy subtly demonstrated her strength every day by modeling what was important and the seriousness of completing a task once started.

In contrast, the lack of male role models in my early life is glaringly apparent. My father, Stephen Earl Thompson, was nonexistent, having long left my life before I was out of infancy. Dana's father passed away and took no part in his life or mine either. And Gus only imparted lessons on how not to conduct oneself as a grown man.

So, here I am—a man. A success in the eyes of many, but a man who has been raised by women. I reflect on my generational transcendence out of a legacy laced with poverty, alcoholism, and abuse and realize that my success is largely attributed to the women in my life. I often contemplate whether my success is largely attributable to my being male. Would I have made it if I was Stephanie instead of

Stephen? What if I were a female and had to vigilantly protect my body from potential predators, as my mother, aunts, and sisters have done? Would I have had the means or psychic wherewithal to pursue my education and career?

I also cannot ignore the fact that my mother ultimately bore seven children with five different men, men who were quickly taken out of the picture by their own volition or by untimely death or by imprisonment. I must acknowledge the fact that as much as I might want to blame my mother for the many hardships I had to endure, I must also lay blame on these missing fathers. Why was it so easy for these men to forsake their own children?

Many times over the years, my sorrow turned toward anger at Brenda. I was enraged that she could just pick up and leave all five of us in that motel room. I could not understand how she never once tried to find us, never once called us, never once wrote to us. To have one's primary relationship shattered with no attempts at repair was incredibly difficult for me to accept.

Writing this story has enabled me to better accept my feelings for Brenda. As I began to tell my story, and accept my own mistakes and flaws, it occurred to me that I am in no position to judge Brenda. I can judge her by the things she did that directly impacted me and my siblings. But did I really know her story? Did I ever think of the pain, loss, and hurt that she may have suffered? Without knowing her full story, I cannot sit in judgment.

I can only presume, given what I witnessed of her life—drug abuse, prostitution, emotional and physical abuse at the hands of many men, extreme poverty—that Brenda experienced a great deal of shame during her lifetime. It may have been that leaving her children in that motel room also filled her with shame. Could it be that she was not mentally, emotionally, or financially able to care for her five young ones? Maybe.

And maybe she hoped that the authorities would find us and provide us with the care that we so desperately needed. Maybe she thought that without her we could find a stable home. Perhaps she knew that to stay on the same trajectory as her own could ultimately lead us to a much worse outcome than abandoning us to an uncertain but possibly better future.

Was her pain so deep, her shame so bitter, that she could never bring herself to speak to Dana and me again? Maybe she hoped that if her shame facilitated our success then it would be worth it. I don't know and never will know. I have resigned myself to accepting that I do not know her story and so it would be unfair of me to judge her. We all fail at different times. We all have shame that is shelved or deeply buried.

Brenda walked away from that motel room leaving her five children inside. She closed the door behind her and, after giving me one last look as she held tightly to a black trash bag, she turned the corner, never to lay eyes on me again. The bright Nevada sun, high above her, must have warmed her brown skin on that crisp winter morning as she turned her back on us. Did she turn that corner and lean against the cinder block building and fall to her knees crying because of what she had just done?

I believe she understood the implications of what she was doing that day. I am sure the consequences of her many poor decisions in life had finally caught up to her, rendering them inescapable in that small, dark motel room. Maybe she agonized over this decision for weeks and days or even years before that fateful day. Only Brenda understands the pain of making the decision to leave her five children behind, knowing that she was never coming back.

When Brenda closed that motel door, she was not just closing it on that part of her life; she was also shutting off the possibility of any future with us, irrevocably severing ties between us and her family as well. She could not have any of her family be a part of our lives either. Brenda insisted that Gus bring Dana and me back to California because she was determined to keep us away from her previous life and family in Ohio. Years later I would learn that my Aunt Ouida had asked Brenda if she could take Dana and me out of foster care and become our guardian. Brenda would not allow her to do so. Maybe Brenda was crying when she saw Brian and Tierra all those years later not just because she missed them but because she had wanted them to stay in Reno away from their father, Gus.

Although my story is one of abandonment, I never permitted that event to define who I was or who I envisioned myself becoming. I had no personal shame about the event, although it was unbearably painful. True embarrassment was my walk of shame down that dark highway guiding my four younger siblings to safety or standing in line at a shelter hoping for a hot meal. I occasionally get embarrassed, but I am immune to allowing that to affect my character. Gina once said to me about my high school days, "You would try anything. You were not afraid." She was right. What could I possibly be afraid of losing?

I did have a deep distrust of people and words for a very long time. I believed that people were always trying to get something from me, and I assumed that all adults struggled with issues of addiction, abuse, and neglect. Kathy really changed that for me. She took the first steps in helping me gain the courage to reveal my vulnerabilities and to open myself up to begin to trust and rely on others. After discovering that I could share my feelings without being taken advantage of, I soon began to allow myself to become more vulnerable and opened myself up to asking for help and relying on others.

I never romanticized that Brenda was out there somewhere searching for us. I never expected to receive a random Christmas card from her or a letter explaining why she left. I never looked up in the stands when I was playing football to see if Brenda was there, surreptitiously watching me on the field as she silently cheered me—her firstborn son—on. We were not going to get any knocks on our door from Brenda saying, "I am so sorry. Can we go grab a cup of coffee and talk?" By not contacting me or Dana, she gave us no hope of a reunion, no hope for closure.

I think Brenda gave me something that day in our dark, cramped motel room. It was a gift. Not a present wrapped in pretty ribbons and shiny paper but a gift that was disguised. I unwrapped it and took great care of it. I did not leave it behind in a motel room like that Rubik's Cube. I did not leave it on the living room floor like children often do once Christmas day has ended. I kept my gift clean and nice. I put it away when I was not playing with it, and I did not let others damage or destroy it. Brenda's unplanned gift to me was breaking the generational cycle of poverty, neglect, and drug abuse. I wish it had been wrapped more carefully. Maybe with a real goodbye, a hug, or even a kiss. Brenda's unplanned gift to me was a new beginning, which eventually provided me with a new family. Unwittingly, she left me a new beginning and a new life.

RENO

THE BIGGEST LITTLE CITY IN THE WORLD

Hotel Goodbyes

DEDICATION: FOR MY SONS

My son Carson had a third-grade assignment several years ago to create his family tree. Carson, being the curious person he is, was eager to learn more about his ancestry.

Penelope can trace her family to the American frontiersman, Davy Crockett. Her family has a family Bible that dates back to the 1600s, including the history of each relative who has lived in the United States since the seventeenth century. Fascinating stuff.

Carson interviewed me about my heritage. I told him about Grandma Kathy's background, her mother, and her mother's mother. My half of his family tree was lopsided next to Penelope's.

In hindsight, I realized I was passive with my answers. My son was not satisfied. So, a couple of days later, Carson sat next to his mother on the couch and asked me, "Why don't you look like Grandma Kathy? I explained that when I was young, I lived in an orphanage, and then Grandma Kathy asked me to live with her, Aunt Gina, and Uncle Vince.

"So why didn't Dana live with you and Grandma?" he asked.

I didn't want to answer. It's complicated and is very much a part of my life that I have filed away. But he kept asking, so I answered his questions.

And then he asked the big question, "What happened to your real mother, Daddy?"

I hesitated. "She left me," I said. "She left me, your uncles, and aunt in a motel room, and we never saw her again."

Carson looked up at me with the eyes of an eight-year-old in disbelief. He immediately started to cry and hugged his mother. My son could not believe the story or imagine how hard it must have been.

I've never forgotten that moment and the expression on Carson's face, and the impact of my words. At that moment, I knew I owed my sons the facts of my life.

It's taken some time, but I've documented my story, life, and family without worrying about how it might appear or reflect on those whose truths I've shared as part of my truth.

For my boys, I needed to convey my learnings, discoveries, and what had brought me to my present life. I needed to show them how special people guided me along the way.

In writing my memoir, I want my sons to know it wasn't the abandonment but the journey that shaped and molded me. I want Quincy and Carson never to worry their parents will desert them. I want them to know we will always care for them and be here for them.

In writing my memoir, I want them to appreciate their opportunities and value their friends and family, too. I want them to realize that another's failings or baggage is not theirs to carry.

In writing my memoir, I hope to ensure that I do not measure them against the challenges of my life. They aren't following in my footsteps, they are taking their own steps, and I'll always be here to guide them as others have guided me.

This book is for you, my sons.